Praise for *l*

"In this graceful, penetrating guide to the forgotten virtues, Elizabeth Kelly introduces readers to a series of lesser-known holy women whose paths to heaven are both eminently relatable and utterly unique. *Love like a Saint* challenges today's women to see the story that Jesus is weaving in our own lives, and to respond to his grace with the small, daily acts of love that are the stepping stones to eternal joy."
—COLLEEN CARROLL CAMPBELL, award-winning author of *The Heart of Perfection, My Sisters the Saints*, and *The New Faithful*.

"Today, as in every age, the greatest need of our world is saints. Liz Kelly paints the portraits of real women who sought virtue and holiness in their daily lives. In a practical way, she draws out the interconnectedness of the virtues as they build upon and illuminate each other. This book will be a source of encouragement and hope for those pursuing holiness in their own lives. I recommend it wholeheartedly."
—THE MOST REV. ANDREW H. COZZENS, S.T.D., D.D., Auxiliary Bishop of the Archdiocese of St. Paul and Minneapolis

"*Love like a Saint* is a beautiful deep dive into various holy women who have been incredibly inspirational examples of a surrendered heart to God. This abandoned hope in our Lord is transformative to our every day, when we recognize that he is the source of all our holiness, our virtue, and our onward journey in the spiritual life. This book will lead you to a deepening love of virtue—not one of obligation, but a desire to look more and more like the Lord. I am so grateful to Liz for writing such an important and vital book to our spiritual journey, and I am even more grateful for the lives of these women who so exemplify love of our Lord."

—JENNA GUIZAR, founder and creative director of Blessed Is She

"This new book will inspire many to live the life of holiness and peace that we are all called to as disciples of Jesus. In the *Catechism of the Catholic Church*, we read: 'Within the communion of the Church, the Holy Spirit "distributes special graces among the faithful of every rank" for the building up of the Church. Now, "to each is given the manifestation of the Spirit for the common good"' (951). Liz Kelly introduces us to and invites us to taste and savor the power of real mutual friendship with the saints as they intercede for us and with us. Through these mutual friendships, we are honored to claim a deeper participation in our own unique charisms that bless the Church as Christ's Mystical Body.

—FR. JOHN HORN, SJ, author of *Heart Speaks to Heart: A Review of Life and Healing Prayer*

"Being with holy women is a way to enter into deeper friendship with God. I found each of these chapters to be a launching point into rich and intimate prayer times."

—MARCIE STOKMAN, founder of Well-Read Mom and author of *The Well-Read Mom: Read More. Read Well*

"I love, love, love *Love like a Saint!* Through captivating storytelling and frequent quippy turns of a phrase, Elizabeth Kelly invites you into intimate friendship with some spunky, spirited, prayerful, and patient holy women. In sharing her story, Kelly links arms with you and takes you on a virtuous journey while at the same time connecting you to saintly women whose struggles and littleness became joy and greatness through their complete surrender to the love of God. The result—an extraordinary band of Christian friendship that inspires you to courageously embrace being the saint God has called you to be—no matter how unpredictable your path to sainthood may be. A brilliant book for anyone who could use a few colorful companions on this journey!"

—KELLY WAHLQUIST, founder of WINE: Women in the New Evangelization, author of *Created to Relate: God's Design for Peace and Joy* and editor of *Walk in Her Sandals: Experiencing Christ's Passion through the Eyes of Women, Gaze Upon Jesus: Experiencing Christ's Childhood through the Eyes of Women,* and *Called By Name: 365 Daily Devotions for Catholic Women.*

ELIZABETH M. KELLY

LOVE LIKE A SAINT

Cultivating Virtue with Holy Women

theWORD
among us®
press

Published by The Word Among Us Press
7115 Guilford Drive, Suite 100
Frederick, Maryland 21704
wau.org

25 24 23 22 21   2 3 4 5 6

ISBN: 978-1-59325-551-0
eISBN: 978-1-59325-550-3

Design by Suzanne Earl

Cover art: "Mary and Elizabeth" (tempera on board) by Dorothy Webster Hawksley (1884-1970), The Maas Gallery, London.

Made and printed in the United States of America

Library of Congress Control Number:
2021901832

For "my women," especially
Pamela
Kathy
Monica
Jeanette
Sarah
Anne
and Kirsten

Christians who are sent into the world are put on the path with authority and with the powers to convince, but these powers do not refer to the ones sent; they refer only to the Lord who is proclaimed. The same can be said in relation to faith, hope, and love, insofar as they are meant to draw people's attention to God's form in the word.

—Hans Urs von Balthasar, *Love Alone Is Credible*

TABLE OF CONTENTS

INTRODUCTION

*The life of each saint is the life of
Jesus Christ; it is a new Gospel.*
—*Jean-Pierre de Caussade*[1]

When I was a kid, I had a rather ghoulish fascination with St. Rita of Cascia. The real and important story behind St. Rita of Cascia—what made her a saint—was a tale of patience, obedience, and her ability to bring about peace at a time of great unrest between two warring political factions. But what captured my attention were the images portraying her later in life with a thorn protruding from her forehead.

She was in her sixties when it appeared one day, while she was deep in prayer before the Blessed Sacrament. She had longed to join her suffering to the suffering Christ. She had been thirty-some years in a monastery, living a simple daily obedience in religious life before she was visited with such an unusual phenomenon. Still, it was the thorn that captured my attention. To my childhood imagination, I could not reconcile how it could be a sign of holiness. And if it was, would it mean a thorn would erupt from my forehead if I let God have his way with me? I was fascinated and repulsed at the same time. I was a child.

Of course, it's not uncommon for some of this reticence toward holiness—or what we imagine holiness to be—to follow us into adulthood, along with the ignorance that accompanies it. I have no desire to die in the gas chamber—like St. Edith Stein. Or to develop a debilitating, merciless disease—like Blessed Benedetta Bianchi Porro. Or to marry a relentlessly abusive and unfaithful man—like Blessed Elizabetta Canori Mora. Or to gulp down cancerous pus—like St. Catherine of Siena. Do you?

Does this mean that heroic virtue is far out of our grasp? To this point, the great Carmelite master Wilfrid Stinissen is exceptionally helpful. He writes:

> It can be risky to read the lives of saints *if* we do it with the intention of imitating them in every detail. What the life of a saint can inspire in us is the will to live in the same total obedience and surrender, in the same openness to the Spirit's constantly new impulses. It is fascinating to see what God can do with a person who is willing to follow the Lamb wherever he goes (Rev 14:4). But it is good to know that the Lamb is totally "unpredictable" and that there is a new, surprising path for each person.[2]

It goes without saying that growing in holiness is not easy and is often uncomfortable. Still, it should hearten us to know that our embodiment of sainthood bears a completely unique imprint. There will be no saint exactly like you in heaven. What you bring to sainthood—however small, or hidden, or uneventful it may seem—has been imparted uniquely to you. Only you, with the grace of God, can bring it to fruition.

I hope this idea frees you to become exactly who you are meant to be without the poison of comparing yourself with others. We do not compete with the great saints; rather, we situate ourselves beside them, shoulder to shoulder.

Are there days when the grace of heaven will carry you? Certainly. It was designed to do so. Are there moments when your holiness will bring a tiny bit of glory to the kingdom? Most assuredly. You were designed to do so. Will there be times when others rely on your hope to carry them through their difficulties and doubts? Indeed. No one enters the gates of heaven alone; we always get there together, as a Church.

This project grew out of a twofold interest: to introduce you to some truly spectacular women in the Church—a few already recognized as saints, a few under consideration for sainthood, and a few who aren't but are surely holy nonetheless—and to offer a kind of living workbook on the virtues. Growth and mastery in the virtues is a long and exacting process, so I didn't feel the need to cover every possible virtue, just a few that are important in the lives of women today.

I've included some questions, for small-group discussion or journaling, and suggestions for praying with Scripture based on each virtue. You might consider praying with a verse for a week and then moving on to the next. Take your time—and take heart: even St. Ignatius of Loyola reported having to pray for a grace for nine months before he received it. St. Catherine of Siena once remarked that "judgment" was the last sin to leave her and the most pernicious against which she had to fight to achieve virtuous victory. Indeed, the women you will meet in these pages might be more like you than you know, and I trust that they will keep you close company on your journey toward greater virtue.

It's helpful to remember too that the virtues thrive within us as a family—charity with humility, poverty with simplicity, silence with faith. So while I do want to highlight one or two virtues that each of these women embodied heroically, it should be understood that they exhibited many virtues heroically. No virtue stands alone. Some are infused, like faith, hope, and love, and we must strive for others more formally. But they all intertwine, depending upon and flowing from one another; and like the spices in a really good curry, they work better the longer they intermingle.

You will be heartened to know that St. Rita and I made peace not long ago. A group from Church of the Divine Child in Detroit, Michigan, wanted to bring me in to speak, but they didn't quite have the funds to manage a stipend, airfare, and hotel. The woman who invited me, Andrea, agreed we would continue to pray and wait to see what happened.

Maybe a day later, another woman called me from a different parish in Detroit. They were looking for a speaker for an event that just happened to fall the night before the Divine Child event. They would be eager to split airfare if that were possible.

Little did I know, Andrea had been praying a novena to St. Rita, that her parish could find a way to bring me to Detroit.

The woman who called from the other parish? Her name was Rita, and she worked for—you guessed it—St. Rita Catholic Church.

The saints, just like the Lord, have infinite patience with us. They will never give up on us, they will never stop praying for us, and when we ask them with a sincere heart that is abandoned to heaven, they will stop at nothing to help us love like a saint.

I

VENERABLE

Anne de Guigné

1911–1922

Obedience

There's probably a little bit of Eve in all of us, some little corner all too willing to be beguiled by the smooth invitation to disobey. "Go ahead, take the apple. Your eyes will be opened, and you'll become like gods!"

Of course, we know how that turned out for Eve. No doubt there are a few "apple moments" in your life that you wish you could take back. I have certainly entertained a few regrettable apples I wish I could unpick.

Our culture doesn't help. It could easily be argued that obedience has fallen out of fashion. It's mocked as a weakness or a lack of self-worth, as something to be medicated, not celebrated. Rebellion has taken its place as a virtue. Certainly, well-placed rebellion can be virtuous, but it must be wielded first by a well-trained obedience. It's all too easy to mistake my willfulness and wanting-what-I-want-when-I-want-it for a kind of pious insurrection.

In a culture that values independence and bowing to the desires of the self above all else, it's not entirely unreasonable to ask, how can obedience as a virtue apply to me? I live in the real world, not the nursery.

Some years ago I was asked by an employer to do work that would directly contradict Church teaching. In a wild panic, I ran to my priest—an exceptionally brilliant man, holder of at least two PhDs—and told him my dilemma. He smiled and said, "I know who we'll call." Within minutes we were on the phone with another priest, a specialist in the ethics of this area of Church teaching.

His confidence—in the Church, in the truth—was striking. Not an ounce of panic or worry in him. In fact, he almost laughed when I told him what I was being asked to do. "Oh, no, you definitely cannot support that," he said. He then added knowingly, "You have the truth on your side," as if to say, "Daughter, you are completely protected."

He talked me through the short argument and then e-mailed me a more thorough bullet list, working through the issue in greater detail. It was as plain as day—the work was immoral—and I had zero intention of doing it. But to tell my boss. Would I be fired? How would I pay my mortgage? Could I really do what I knew the Father was asking me to do?

Walking back to my office, something unexpected started to rise up in me, something like joy. It swaddled my fear. Such a strange pairing, but I felt that I understood the agony in the garden for the first time in my adult life. Anticipating the horror that lay ahead, Jesus asked his Father, "Let this cup pass from me; yet, not as I will, but as you will" (Matthew 26:39). There was no way he would disobey his Father, no moment he would even consider it. Obedience to the Father's will sat at the very core of his being, and as it turns out, it was the seed of joy, flourishing, and unstoppable glory.

I won't lie; it was a rough few months for me, consulting attorneys and stumbling through some uncomfortable conversations with my boss and human resources. But in the end, the law was on my side, and I was not forced to do work that would be immoral.

Fr. Wickham writes, "The freely committed obedience of adult Christians is *to God*, not mainly to other human beings, whatever rank," though sometimes we are guided by those of rank onto the best path. He adds that this will always call for "continued growth in maturity . . . [and] a great deal of prayer."[3]

And I'll say this: God is constantly rewarding that tiny act of obedience in the thoroughly satisfying work that I have now. Obedience—even in the littlest things—always results in flourishing and immoveable joy.

Indeed, obedience is not a virtue we leave behind in the nursery but one that we must take pains to cultivate into a robust maturity. And however ironically, it is one we will learn a great deal about from "the apostle of the nursery," Anne de Guigné.

The Little Girl Who Lived in a Castle

Anne's family home, Château de la Cour, overlooked the expanse of the gorgeous Lake of Annecy, situated in the alpine region of southeastern France, just south of Geneva, Switzerland. It was a bucolic and breathtaking place in which to grow up, and Anne enjoyed the benefits of a secure, well-educated family who spent their winters in a second home in Cannes.

Anne was the eldest daughter of Jacques, Count de Guigné, a well-read and deeply prayerful Catholic, and Antoinette de Charette, equally devout. Antoinette traced her lineage not only to St. Louis, King of France, but also to General de Charette, who fought for Pope Pius IX in Rome under the banner of the Sacred Heart.[4] An auspicious beginning for Anne, to say the least.

Anne, also called Nenette, was followed by Jacques (Jojo), Madeleine (LeLeine), and Marie Antoinette (Marinette), all born in close succession. It's not uncommon for an eldest child to develop some distaste for the arrival of number two. After all, they have been the sole proprietor of Mother's lap for some time, and now there's an interloper. Such was the case with little Nenette when her brother JoJo arrived about a year after her own birth.

One day, upon witnessing her mother kissing the infant, Nenette found some sand and tried to rub it into JoJo's eyes. Fortunately she was intercepted before she could render any real damage with her chubby toddler fingers. Indeed, from infancy Anne's life was marked not by the virtue of obedience—as some hagiographers might invite us to believe about their subjects—but by an unusually strong will. She was a precocious soul, mature beyond her years and full of a bossy, creative kind of mischief that must have made disciplining her difficult.

When she was a very young child, for example, a seriously ill Anne threw a fit when a doctor tried to examine her, flailing arms and legs at his advance. When he tried to hold her down, she declared, "Take your hat and go!"[5] Examples of this kind of behavior in her early life were not uncommon, earning her the playful title "the little tyrant."

Like most of us, Anne's strengths could also be her weaknesses. She was a born leader and sometimes pushy; she was loving but also jealous; she was deeply intelligent and creative, which sometimes resulted in impressive feats of naughtiness, such as going to remarkable and inventive lengths to steal a forbidden chocolate.

A delightful tale comes from the day her youngest sister was baptized. Anne was around four years old. Because of a dangerous cold spell, the family received permission for the baptism to take place at home. One of Anne's biographers recounts it this way:

It was a great day for Anne; she felt she had "come of age," in fact, for her mother decided that she should be allowed to stand as godmother. Feeling full of importance she made the responses very gravely; but what most impressed her was the fact that she was now responsible for Marinette's welfare. This was very much to Anne's taste, and she did not stop to distinguish between spiritual and temporal care! No one in the house had a chance of forgetting that the baby had a godmother. All that day Anne hovered about, trying to get hold of her spiritual charge, and at last succeeded in reaching the crib when the nurse was not looking. But good nurses have eyes in the backs

of their heads, and this one looked around in time to catch
the godmother just as she was getting the baby into her arms.

"My darling, you mustn't touch her. Little girls can't look
after babies!"

Anne drew herself up with dignity: "They can on a Baptism
day," she retorted. "I'm her godmother."[6]

It's hard not to admire the fact that a young child would
have so strong a sense of herself and take her duties so earnestly. Her earliest years are filled with such tales—Anne taking
charge, and beware anyone who would challenge her.

From Little Tyrant to Little Lamb

In the early twentieth century, before he'd married, Anne's
father had served in the Chasseurs Alpins, an elite mountain
infantry. He retired from military service to take up family life,
but when World War I broke out, he reenlisted. He was injured
several times and had to return home to recuperate on two
occasions. There Anne, age four, served as "nurse," bringing
him books and fluffing his pillows with all the officiousness
her family had come to expect from her.

In February of 1915, the count was injured so severely that
he required surgery in a Lyon hospital. Anne's mother took her
to visit him, and one wonders what influence such an experience—seeing so many wounded from war—may have had
on little Anne.

Once the count was reasonably recovered, he courageously
returned to war a fourth time, only to be mortally wounded on

July 24, 1915. The news reached Anne's family four days later, and it was her mother who explained to Anne that her father was lost in war. His body would not be recovered by the family, only adding to the strangeness and confusion of his passing.

Though she was only four, her father's death was a turning point for Anne. As she watched her mother grieve, a radical internal shift began to take place. She would never have expressed it this way, but it seems she was falling in love with Jesus so profoundly and so compellingly that her short life would become a credible testimony to Jesus' statement in John's Gospel: "If you love me, you will keep my commandments" (John 14:15). She began to approach her life with the simple genius that so often flourishes in children. Her biographer writes:

> Anne was a practical little soul. She realized now that to reach God we must please him and to please him we must be good and that the surest way for a little girl to be good is by pleasing her mother. So she set to work first of all to comfort her mother in every way she could. All day long she tried to be thoughtful and to remember the things she had been told to do—and tried to make the others remember too, for the old instinct of command was not dead! If she herself had started on the way of perfection, she meant to carry them all along with her.
>
> "You must be good, Jojo, because Mother is sad," she used to whisper to her noisy little brother, who was more inclined to listen now that there were no more tempers to be feared from Nenette. . . . All she thought of was how to please the others, so of course there were no more tempers, no selfishness, because

she no longer wanted to get her own way but to make them happy and above all to keep them good.[7]

And Jesus was ever near her to help. Just two weeks after the death of her father, Anne attended a solemn Mass with her aunt and grandmother. Her aunt continued to pray awhile after Mass, and concerned that they had stayed too long for the little girl, she said, "Perhaps we have been here a little too long; do you want me to give you my Rosary?" Anne replied, "Oh no, I am speaking with the little Jesus in the Tabernacle."[8]

Indeed, Anne was developing an unusual sense of the presence of Jesus in the Blessed Sacrament. Her thoughts, even at such a young age, often turned to the Eucharist and the best ways she could make the heart of Jesus happy.

Anne's mother enrolled her in catechism classes, at which she excelled, and she was ready to receive her First Communion at the age of six. The local bishop disapproved when he saw such a young child being put forward, but he was persuaded when Anne's teachers and confessor told him that they were convinced of her preparedness. The bishop made arrangements for the superior of the local Jesuits to grill her rigorously, to see if in fact this was the case. When the superior saw her and saw how young she was, he said, "Really, it is rather absurd to present such a baby."

As the interview went on, however, the priest became more and more impressed with Anne. He did not question her in any kind of order but at random, at length, and with some complexity. It wasn't long before he was convinced that Anne was ready to receive the sacrament.

One exchange in particular stands out. The priest asked Anne, "What's your chief fault?"

Anne replied, "Pride, and disobedience too."

Her reply impressed the priest, and he encouraged her in obedience. But then, in a moment made for arguing the cause of a saint, he asked the child, "When does Jesus obey?"

"At Mass," Anne answered.

"What words does he obey?" the priest continued.

"He obeys the priest when he says, 'This is my Body, this is my Blood,'" Anne replied.

After some time, the priest emerged from the interview with Anne and said, "I wish you and I were as well prepared to receive Our Lord as this little girl is."[9]

On the day of her First Communion, Anne wrote a little note and placed it on the altar. It read, "My Jesus, I love You, and to please You, I resolve to obey You always." And she meant it.

The Beauty in Obedience

The theme of obedience hovered over Anne's short life like a gentle but protective angel. The motto of Anne's First Communion retreat was "Obedience is the sanctity of children," and she took this to heart.

Nota bene: It wasn't that Anne was simply obedient; many children afraid of punishment will obey. Rather her motivation for obedience entered the realm of the mystical. Anne was not trying to avoid punishment; she was trying to avoid wounding the heart of someone she deeply loved, Jesus. Her obedience joined her to the obedience of Jesus, who came to do the Father's will. Nothing was more important to her. Her sensitivity to the sadness that sin evokes in the Sacred Heart (her eyes would well up with tears when she heard stories of the sins of others) and to the joy that obedience to the Father brings was like a window through which she read every soul she encountered.

This was no more evident than with her siblings, JoJo in particular. He was a typical, rambunctious, sometimes naughty little boy. When the usual entreaties for better behavior didn't work, Anne would tell him, "Remember, JoJo, you're going to Communion tomorrow." As if to say, "You couldn't possibly want to offend Jesus in the Blessed Sacrament, could you?"

One time JoJo got ahold of Anne's favorite china doll and started tossing it in the air and catching it again. Anne begged him to stop, fearing he would drop it. JoJo kept at it, tossing the doll higher and higher until at last he dropped it, and it crashed all over the floor. JoJo was remorseful, and Anne forgave him immediately, but she didn't stop there.

Her mother was out, and Anne waited up until late in the evening for her mother's return. Through drooping eyelids, she begged her mother not to scold JoJo, saying, "Oh, Mother, I didn't want to go to sleep till I told you. Please don't scold JoJo; he didn't do it on purpose."

There were times she would finish JoJo's prayers for him when he was too sleepy to do so. On the occasions when he gave in to naughty behavior, Anne would retreat to a corner to pray for him. She played endless games with him, even giving him horseback rides for hours, though they caused her some serious discomfort. She coached JoJo on the joys of his First Communion, telling him, "You can't imagine how lovely it is!"

Anne constantly encouraged her siblings not only to be good but also to be generous and to make little sacrifices on behalf of others. She often invited her little brood, who grew to adore their tender-hearted older sister, to give up a dessert or some other little treat "for poor sinners." And this from a child who'd previously invented ingenious ways to steal sweets!

Anne loved the poor, and on at least one occasion, she enlisted the help of her siblings to put on a fundraiser for the less fortunate. Their lovely bazaar included delectables and trinkets that Anne had made, as well as the children's treats and sweets that they had saved for the event.

Beyond setting a tireless example of obedience and small daily sacrifices for her siblings, Anne loved to pray for the conversion of the most intractable of sinners. She took on "cases" as a little spiritual doctor. She often asked the sisters at her school to give her "a big sinner" to take care of. And then the battle began.

Nenette prayed and made more sacrifices than ever until her sinner came back to God. In this way she caught many "big fishes," as she called them, for her Jesus.[10] Madame de Guigné once remarked, "Nothing would stop her when she meant to save a soul. She would sacrifice herself in countless little ways and never lost a chance of offering something to God for her poor sinner."[11]

Well beyond the nursery, Anne's love for Jesus radiated from her prayerful heart in ways that were impossible to ignore. Her life is replete with stories like this: One day, a woman, a nonbeliever, entered a church and found Anne praying. Observing the beautiful expression on Anne's face, the woman converted on the spot, saying, "Never again will I say there is no God."[12]

Children in church observed Anne looking as though she were engaged in the most engrossing, most splendid conversation with someone she dearly loved. Her nanny, on finding her kneeling in a corner, asked her what she was doing and Anne replied, "Oh, I was only thanking Jesus for being so kind as to come into my heart."

Anne also developed an unusually strong awareness of heaven. She spoke of eternity often and with joy.

Anne's mother would naturally grow solemn, remembering the loss of her beloved husband whenever there were reminders of war—seeing men in uniform or encountering soldiers who'd served with her husband. It was then that Anne would whisper something hopeful to her mother. "Daddy is in heaven, and he is so happy," or, "Remember, Daddy is with Jesus, and we will all be together again soon."

As it turned out, Anne would be reunited with her father much sooner than anyone knew or would wish.

Going to the Angels

There have been many accounts of adult saints understanding that their deaths were drawing near; it's rarer to name children who were entrusted with this special knowledge. Yet Anne seemed to know and to carry this knowing in her person like a beam of light. One nun remarked on it this way: "One [could] see Jesus in her eyes. It was unforgettable, the strange mixture of innocence and gravity in those clear eyes."[13]

Others observed her leaving Confession and said that her whole person seemed to be transfigured, transformed into grace itself. Another child—a friend who left for a trip some months before Anne's death—said she was certain she would not see Anne again. "I am sure God is going to take her," she said. "She doesn't seem to belong to this world anymore."

Beginning at about the age of eight, Anne suffered from chronic headaches, the result of some weakness in her spine. Though they caused her such severe pain that she could not study in school, she never complained but lay still to wait quietly for relief.

These headaches returned with renewed ferocity in December of 1921, when Anne was ten. Just after Christmas of that year, she was diagnosed with meningitis. The pain in her back and head was so severe at times that it contorted her beautiful little face—something she struggled against because she knew it upset her mother to see her in so much pain. Still she was gracious with everyone who came to visit or to care for her, thanking them, insisting that those who nursed her throughout the night would please rest or at least have a sweet treat.

On the Feast of the Holy Innocents—and how extraordinarily apropos—Anne's priest heard her Confession and then asked if she would like to receive Holy Communion.

"Oh, *yes*," she sighed.

He would write some years later, "Never shall I forget that word. The whole desire of her soul was in it."[14]

In her last weeks, the pain was crippling. Eventually her lungs deteriorated to such a degree that she suffered terrible bouts of near suffocation that lasted for hours. But all the while she remained at peace and without complaint, offering her sufferings for "dear sinners." Her exquisite relationship with the Lord—intimate, knowing, and without the slightest fear of death—was a witness to the entire household, to visitors, and to those who took care of her.

Not long after Anne received the Anointing of the Sick,

> Madame de Guigné bent over the child's bed and whispered to her: "You *have* been brave, darling. This will comfort the Heart of Our Lord and win over some of your sinners." The torture had wrung no word from Anne, but now she gasped with joy. "Oh, Mother, I'm so glad. If it does that, I will bear lots more."[15]

As Anne entered into her final days, confined to her room, she seemed to have a number of notable divine visitors, including her guardian angel. She repeated the Act of Hope and the Hail Holy Queen. When her little body was completely exhausted with pain, she asked permission to die. She turned to the nun who was nursing her and asked, "May I go to the angels?" When the nun gave her blessing, Anne replied "Thank you, thank you!"

Even her last act on this earth was marked by holy obedience. In observing her mother's deep grief, the doctor leaned over Anne and asked her if she wouldn't look at her mother just once more. Her biographer recorded the moment this way: "And Anne, obedient even in death, lifted her eyelids with a last effort and looked at her mother with a look that is burned into her soul forever. Then she sank into that sleep from which the Angels were to wake her."[16]

She died January 14, 1922, at the age of ten.

"And a Little Child Shall Lead Them"

Anne's story on this earth was robust but short, a happy prelude to her eternal story, which continues to flourish. Not surprisingly, it was JoJo who perhaps realized this most quickly.

In those first hours, when Anne's little body was still in the family home, JoJo sat for a long while, confiding in her, telling his mother, "I have so much more to tell Nenette." Then, all at once, he began darting around collecting little prayer books, rosaries, and other holy objects scattered throughout the house. He touched each one to Anne's hand, proclaiming to those in the house, "One day you will be very glad I did this!" None too concerned with the process and rules around canonization, JoJo was creating relics.

Many conversions and healings have been attributed to Anne's intercession, but none quite so moving as the conversion of one intractable sinner from her own parish. He was an "earthy soul" and far from God. As he lay dying, the nuns and the priest who cared for him begged him to make his peace with God. He refused. This went on for some time—the entreaty of those who cared for him and his absolute refusal to acknowledge God.

Then his attendants turned to Anne and begged her intercession on behalf of this "poor sinner." Just moments before his death, after he had lain unconscious for days, the man woke up, asked for a priest, and offered his Confession. He then received Holy Viaticum "with the fervor of an angel."[17]

Many of the virtues have suffered under the strains of a culture that values independence above all things; obedience has suffered near annihilation. Perhaps this is why heaven has sent us a child to model it for us. Maybe we simply couldn't learn this exquisite and nuanced lesson from an adult.

Anne was declared venerable by Pope John Paul II on March 3, 1990.

Venerable Anne, pray for us, that our love for the Lord would ever increase and that our sensitivity to the sorrow of sin would drive us to obey as you did, with gentleness, generosity, and a desire to always please the heart of heaven. Amen.

Anne at ten years old

IN HER OWN WORDS

Our work is a present that we can give Jesus. So when it seems hard, just think that now you have something for him. Nothing costs much when we love Him.[18]

I will imitate the little Jesus.[19]

My soul is meant for heaven. We take a lot of trouble over dressing our bodies but think much less about our souls. . . . There ought to be: First, cleanness (of soul), which means avoiding sin. Second, proper clothing, that is doing our duty. Third, adornment, which means the good actions that we do of our free will. . . . It depends on me; Mother cannot do the work for me.[20]

FOR JOURNALING

1. What would your life look like if you were to grow in the virtue of obedience? Is there a particular relationship or area in your life that would benefit from a deeper obedience to God?
2. What were the effects of obedience in Anne's life?
3. What might be some of the effects of greater obedience in yours?
4. Getting creative as did little Venerable Anne, what's one act of obedience you could regularly incorporate into your life or the life of your family?
5. Write a prayer asking Venerable Anne's help. Invite your children or grandchildren to do the same.

FOR PRAYER

Asking for the grace of obedience, pray with

1. **Ezekiel 36:22-32:** An obedient heart
2. **Matthew 21:23-32:** Discern the will of God.
3. **John 4:31-38:** My food is to do the will of God.
4. **Romans 5:12-21:** Justified by one man's obedience
5. **Deuteronomy 4:32-40:** A loving response to God's love
6. **Philippians 2:5-11:** Obedient even unto death
7. **1 Corinthians 3:1-9:** We are the Lord's servants.
8. **Acts 5:27-32:** We must obey God, not man.

2

Blessed

Benedetta Bianchi Porro
1936–1964

Friendship and Perseverance

For my niece, Anja

Virtues often appear together in a complementary way—
like two hands folded in prayer. Sometimes this is the
case with perseverance and friendship, as illustrated by the
following story.

Dr. Michael J. Brescia, executive medical director and
cofounder of Calvary Hospitals in the Bronx and Brooklyn,
gave a remarkable account of the power of friendship—of the
simple act of being present, of persisting—in an interview published in the *National Catholic Bioethics Quarterly*:

One day I was leaving for Washington, and I got a call from Metropolitan Hospital. They had a woman they had found under the highway. Could they send her right to Calvary [Hospital]? She had no family; she wasn't speaking. She was filthy, and her name was Angela. So I said, "Okay, we'll take her." And as I was leaving, Angela was coming in; she had a big tumor coming out of her back. She had chopped red hair, no teeth. She had AIDS [and] hepatitis and was draining all kinds of infected material. Of course our cancer care technicians were anxious to go to work on her.

I was in Washington for one day, fighting for funding. When I came back I went upstairs to see her, and I couldn't believe what they'd done. They cleaned her up, worked on her mouth, did her hair, did her nails. She didn't look like she understood anything, but I said, "I'm going to promise you, Angela, that I will see you three times every day." I thought, "Three times a day I'm going to come in and touch you and tell God, 'I'm going there because of my love for you.'"

Six weeks later, I'm coming back from Washington again feeling discouraged. I think, "Oh, I won't go to see her tonight; I'll see her tomorrow." Then I think, "No, I'd better go. I'll feel miserable tonight if I don't go." I go up to the floor, and Angela is dying. So I take off my coat, and I take her hand, put it on my cheek, and I say, "Angela, I'm staying."

Exactly ninety minutes later, I hear, "Dr. Michael, Dr. Michael." I couldn't believe my ears. I jump up, and I've got her now as tightly as I can, and I say, "Angela?" She said, "Dr. Michael, tonight, in a few hours, I'll speak your name to God." She never spoke another word. She closed her eyes and left this earth. [21]

We cannot underestimate the power of friendship, of simply being present to one another, even when circumstances would suggest that it doesn't really matter, it won't make any difference. Neither can we overestimate how profoundly we need this experience of friendship as technology continues to dehumanize and depersonalize so many of our interactions.

But Dr. Brescia's story is an account not only of friendship but also of perseverance, a virtue that needs revisiting.

Looking through Death

Sometimes I think we imagine Jesus on his way to the cross with white-knuckled fists, driven by a fierce yet holy determination. Therefore we think that is the way we must practice perseverance—with clenched fists and through sheer human will, never giving up, never conceding—fight, fight, fighting to the end.

If we understand Christian perseverance in this way, something quite telling happens: we focus on ourselves, on our own effort, leaving Jesus completely out of the equation. And if life hasn't taught us yet, it probably will: this is a fundamentally flawed interpretation of the virtue of perseverance.

In his book *The Real Presence of the Coming Kingdom*, Fr. John Wickham defines Christian perseverance as "the graced ability to continue giving one's deepest heart."[22] That is, giving your heart to heaven, giving your heart to the eternal values that govern it, no matter what might be happening in your life. When I read his definition, I felt I was struck by holy lightning. Perseverance is not simply about struggling to overcome difficulty but about measuring that difficulty against the reality of eternity and depending on God to bring you through it with soul intact.

Fr. Wickham's definition completely reframed the virtue for me. Perseverance is not a white-knuckle kind of virtue. Perseverance doesn't have anything to do with being tough; it has to do with being *generous*. (Think of the promise Dr. Brescia kept to Angela.) Understood in this way, perseverance takes on an open posture—one of open hands, an open heart ready to give and receive according to God's will.

Perseverance is not so much something you conjure; it's something you receive. And more importantly, it places a proper emphasis on God—what God will do—and on your dependence and confidence in *his* generosity to give you this graced ability to continue giving your heart to him no matter what might be happening around you or to you.

Jesus did not walk to Calvary with clenched fists. He walked the Via Dolorosa with an open heart and open hands, into which the Father placed the cross. Christ on the way to Calvary is not tough, resilient, stubborn, dogged; rather, he is given and giving. Giving his heart to the Father, he measured his cross by eternity's scale.

I want that kind of heart, that kind of perseverance. But it sounds mighty painful and a touch frightening.

Fr. Wickham's response is both wise and reasonable. He reminds us, "We cannot lay claim to [perseverance] as . . . due to us because of contributions we have already made. No, it always remains something additional we need to pray for from day to day as we go along." That is, it's a gift. And furthermore,

"It develops a deep level devotion to the ultimate goal. Characteristically, it 'looks through death' to what is beyond all time, and this in turn tends to free a person's heart from present satisfactions."[23]

In other words, perseverance brings *freedom*, freedom to love and to serve.

We think of St. Teresa of Kolkata and the protracted season she suffered without sensing God's presence—the last half of her long life—yet remained faithful to her incredible mission to the poor. Or of St. John of the Cross, who was imprisoned and beaten by his confreres and yet still led a massive reform of the Carmelite Order. Or of Pope St. John Paul II, who continued to lead the Church after being diagnosed with Parkinson's. Drooling and shaken by tremors, he even appeared in public, before crowds. These saints embody a radical kind of perseverance that "looks through death."

People like this, writes Wickham, "chose to be true to values which no short-term, narrowly conceived arguments would countenance. Their fidelity appears to have emerged from considerations deeper than, or beyond, any ordinary reckoning. And their perseverance against all odds must be respected as a special divine grace."[24] It is a grace we can all pray to receive.

Fr. Wickham makes one final, important distinction:

Too many Christians resemble the Prodigal's elder brother, caught up in and bound to a kind of fidelity to rules rather than to persons. The rules are usually good ones as far as they go, but that is not far. As a result, for them to persevere through serious changes of fortune is not really possible. Alter the little social rules and they quickly become lost.[25]

That is, those who persevere do so because they are faithful not to an idea or a principle but to a *Person*. It's a critical distinction because fidelity to *only* rules can crush love and life. Furthermore, this fidelity cannot be sustained. Only fidelity to love, to continue loving in the face of difficulty, to continue giving the deepest part of your heart to a Person—to Jesus—will launch you into eternity.

Dr. Brescia wasn't being faithful to a principle; he was being faithful to a Person. He had given his heart to a deep love, and that love sent him up to Angela's room, one last and most precious time. In that moment, he received a glimpse of eternity through Angela's eyes.

There are those among us who seem created to persevere, whose lives exemplify this "looking through death" to such a degree that they seem to already have one foot in heaven. Benedetta Bianchi Porro is just such a one; you will not regret getting to know her.[26]

An Enchanted Heart

Benedetta was born August 8, 1936, in Dovadola, Forli, Italy. She was the second of six children born to Guido Bianchi Porro, an engineer, and Elsa Giamarchi, a woman who was eager to share her simple yet deep faith with her children.

As an infant, Benedetta contracted polio, which left one of her legs crippled. Later she had to wear a brace to keep her spine from becoming deformed. The brace was tremendously painful, but she bore the pain with unusual strength for a child.

She was an intelligent and happy little girl, with a strong sense of self. A favorite story highlights this.

Benedetta's older brother, Gabriele, had been playing outside with another boy when Benedetta walked by. The little boy said something to the effect of, "Look, here comes the cripple!" In Italy, an older brother is unlikely to let such an insult pass, and Gabriele went to fisticuffs on behalf of his sister. The mothers tried unsuccessfully to break up the fight, until Benedetta limped over and said, "He called me 'the cripple'—what is wrong with that? It's the truth." This apparently put the argument to bed, and the boys went back to playing together.[27]

Benedetta's mother, who "saw in this child something over and above the natural qualities in her other children,"[28] suggested that Benedetta begin keeping a diary. This she did, starting at age five. Her precocious and thoughtful nature is evident in the things she chose to chronicle. She noted when her mother found her naughty and ill-mannered. She kept track of the cherry tree she planted and watered every day and of the games she played with her friends. She catalogued being mesmerized by a sunset or by the men singing in the fields.

One day a calf was born, she wrote, and another day she washed geese. Despite her weakened leg, she built a little house in a cypress tree and often stole away by herself to sit up there and think about the grandeur of the earth. She would often note when she went to Mass and Communion.

She also recorded her experiences during World War II, such as worrying about her mother in Forlì on the days when there were many planes in the sky and bombs were falling. One day she found a hand grenade that Germans had left behind. "How lucky I didn't touch it," she wrote. "God saved me from the danger."[29]

Even in wartime she managed to express childlike wonder. At age seven, she wrote, "The universe is enchanting. It is great to be alive!"[30] And this from a child who not only had to wear a painful brace but also suffered such serious bouts of bronchitis that she had to be hospitalized on several occasions. She suffered from an additional disease, but that would not be diagnosed for some time.

Benedetta was a born student. She loved to study and, at a very early age, determined that she would be a missionary doctor. As a teenager, however, she began losing her hearing, and this placed her dreams of practicing medicine in serious jeopardy. It became more and more difficult for her to hear in the classroom, and occasionally she struggled to make herself understood. She wrote, "What a bad impression I make at times, but it doesn't matter. Maybe one day I will no longer understand anything that other people say, but I will always hear the voice of my soul, and that is the true guide that I must follow."[31]

Despite this growing disability, Benedetta was an excellent and determined student who loved to read Tolstoy and Shakespeare. She was admitted to the University of Milan at the age of seventeen. As she entered university, she wrote, "I face my new studies with new strength: I must fulfill my dream of becoming a physician. I want to live, to fight, to sacrifice myself for all men."[32]

God honored her noble prayer. At first some professors objected to a deaf student, but Benedetta proved to have such a fine mind that she was allowed to continue. She learned to read lips but sometimes, for oral exams, requested written questions, which she could read and then respond to orally. Some of her classmates didn't even realize she was deaf.

Benedetta struggled and sacrificed, but ultimately she did not become a medical doctor. In fact, about the only person she ever diagnosed was herself.

In 1957, after four years of medical studies, Benedetta determined that she suffered with neurofibromatosis, also known as Von Recklinghausen's disease—a diagnosis that her professors and other doctors later confirmed. Extremely rare and incurable, the disease involves—alone or in some combination—tumors in the brain, along the spinal cord, and along the nerves that affect signals between the brain and spinal cord. There are several types of neurofibromatosis; in Benedetta's case, small tumors formed on the nerve centers, progressively destroying them.

Typically, in severe cases, the auditory nerve is the first to be damaged, followed by the optic nerve, and then the other senses are compromised—touch, taste, and smell. Finally, progressive paralysis sets in. This was Benedetta's experience.

Over several years, Benedetta had numerous surgeries. She lost her hearing, her eyesight, her ability to move, her sense of taste, even her sense of touch. She maintained the ability to use her right hand and the capacity to speak, even to sing, though only in a whisper.

Through this extraordinary suffering, Benedetta discovered a new kind of enchantment. She became ever more aware of the richness of her interior life—a life beyond the senses of the body, a life intimately connected with Jesus in his agony.

Little Still Host on the Altar

It was clear that from childhood Benedetta's faith was the central force at work in her life. Despite her increasingly beleaguered body, she continued to give the deepest part of her heart to the Father. For example, at one point she had to have her head shaved before an operation. She later recalled how humiliated she felt. "While they were cutting my hair, I felt like a lamb in the hands of the shearer, and I prayed that the Lord would make me strong and small. I suffered so much, and I asked the Lord to make of me a little sheep in his hands."[33]

As soon as she came out of anesthesia for that particular surgery, she touched her face and realized that the doctor had cut a facial nerve, leaving the left half of her face paralyzed. The surgeon was of course mortified at the error. But in an extraordinary act of charity, Benedetta simply told him: "You did what you could; take my hand and be at peace! It was something that could happen—you are not the Eternal Father!"[34] There were no lawsuits, no recriminations, only her hand offered in peace.

Impressively, Benedetta continued in her studies and completed five years of a six-year medical degree. Occasionally she sneaked out of the house with her nurse, Anna, a constant companion, in order to take an exam. She would take the test and then sneak back into bed so as to avoid worrying her mother.

Benedetta had just one year of school to go when an operation—intended to slow the paralysis of her lower body—only made matters worse. She was no longer able to walk. In 1960 she had to completely give up her studies—a tremendous disappointment for one who longed to be active and to serve.

But while her loved ones helplessly watched her progressive physical deterioration, they also witnessed her spiritual growth. Cloistered in her room, she rarely showed sadness or discouragement. She wrote in this time: "I live everyday life, but how full it seems to me! Life itself seems a miracle to me, and I would like to sing a hymn of praise to him who has given it to me."[35]

Her mother gave her a little canary to keep her company but then worried that Benedetta would see too much of herself in the bird's caged life. Benedetta told her, "Mama, I was never as free as I've been since I've been immobilized here."

As her sensible world was shrinking, she revealed moments of darkness to a few close confidants. They were quick to rally to her aid. A priest friend wrote to her:

> You must never feel useless and alone. Your armchair and your
> bed can become an altar. You are not consuming yourself but
> transforming yourself into a Host on that altar. The shadow
> of the cross extends as far as your room, and you, Jesus and
> Mary, form one heart.[36]

This wise and beautiful counsel settled gently in her soul.

In 1960 Benedetta met a new friend, Nicoletta. Some of those closest to Benedetta came to believe that Nicoletta was sent to serve as a spiritual mother. Their correspondence is a priceless testimony to Christian friendship.

Benedetta wrote to Nicoletta,

> At the moment I am going through a period of great aridity. I feel alone, tired, somewhat humiliated, and without much patience. . . . The worst is that I am not at peace. Pray for me, pray for me. . . . Why is this happening to me? Why is God allowing this?[37]

Nicoletta answered Benedetta:

> Don't force yourself to feel what you believe, or to understand why it is fair that you suffer so much. Don't panic if you seem to be rebelling—this is not important in God's eyes. He knows the truth. Before this vast mystery, He wants only our "yes"; it doesn't matter if we say it badly.[38]

In an incredibly telling reply, Benedetta said, "Bless you for the joy you have obtained for me, a joy too great for me, so unworthy. I was flooded with joy, as though all the oceans were poured into a walnut shell."[39]

From that time on, Benedetta received suffering less as a burden to be heroically carried and more as a mark of divine favor. Jesus called her to share his cross so that she might identify with him. She placed herself entirely in his hands and found her strength in the Gospel, which she read every day, in the letters of Saint Paul, and in the Psalms.

In May 1962, Benedetta took the first of two trips to Lourdes, in a train specially outfitted for the transport of the disabled.

At the hospital, in the bed next to hers, was a twenty-two-year-old woman, Maria, paralyzed much like Benedetta. Maria had come to Lourdes to ask the Immaculate Conception for a miracle. She prayed fervently, but nothing happened.

The day before they were to leave, the two young women found themselves side by side at the Grotto. Maria was sobbing. Benedetta took her hand and pressed it in her own. She said, "Maria, the Madonna is here, looking at you! Speak to her, speak to the Madonna!"

All of a sudden, Maria rose from her stretcher. She gingerly took a few steps, incredulous. And then, delirious with joy, she made her way through the wheelchairs, weeping with emotion and gratitude.

Benedetta was of course happy for this miracle, but very humanly, she felt a pang of sadness that she wasn't healed. In that moment, she decided to abandon herself into the hands of Mary.

One year later, Benedetta returned to Lourdes. This time she would report a healing, but it wasn't a physical one. She wrote of her second trip to Lourdes: "I am aware more than ever of the richness of my condition and I don't desire anything but to continue in it. This has been the miracle of Lourdes for me this year."[40] We could say it was a miracle in perseverance, in continuing to give the deepest part of her heart.

Not long after that, Benedetta had another operation, this time on the optic nerve. The operation left her completely blind, but she asked that no one tell the surgeon, so as not to sadden him. She said, "There is nothing to do but trust in God, with eyes closed. I am in the process of living simplicity, that is, the stripping of the soul. How beautiful it is! One becomes so light and free!"[41]

One of her biographers described Benedetta, from that point on, as "an inaccessible castle, with neither doors nor windows."[42] The only means of communication that she possessed were her voice—though it was so weak that she could barely be heard—and her right hand, where her loved ones signed the alphabet for the deaf. Her room was besieged by visitors who came to encourage her but also to ask for her help.

Benedetta had the gift of spreading joy around her, even with the serious limitations on her capacity to communicate. "They'd come and go in groups of ten and fifteen," said Maria Grazia, one of Benedetta's closest confidants.

> With her mother as interpreter, she was able to communicate with each one. It seemed as though she could read our innermost souls with extreme clarity, even though she couldn't hear or see us. I will always remember her with her hand extended ready to receive the word of God and her brothers and sisters.[43]

Maria suffered terribly watching Benedetta's deterioration, but Benedetta reassured her: "We must accept the mystery, Maria Grazia. What fills us with anguish is asking ourselves 'why'? The Lord gives us as much suffering as we can bear—not more, not less." Her friend would later testify, "I then unexpectedly noticed a great peace enveloped her, as though she felt completely freed from fear and anxiety."[44]

In a letter to Nicoletta, Benedetta expressed this freedom and the profound intimacy she felt with Christ:

My days are long and tiring but at the same time sweet and filled with the light of God. I strive in my exile not to lose my serenity. I recall the shouts of the Apostles when Jesus was walking on the water and said, "It is I, be not afraid." . . . My mother reads and writes all of my letters. I have nothing to offer my Lord, my hands are empty except for a few crumbs of bread; but even here in my bed I feel all the tenderness of spring in full bloom. I offer God all the flowers of the world that have blossomed under His sun. I often think of my last hour and . . . if I am afraid, I will say without shame: "I am afraid, Lord, strengthen me."[45]

Friendship in Letters

In his *Introduction to the Devout Life*, St. Francis de Sales wrote: "Love everyone with a deep love based on charity . . . but form friendships only with those who can share virtuous things with you. The higher the virtues you share and exchange with others, the more perfect your friendship will be."[46]

Benedetta's friendships deeply embodied this principle. Extraordinary bands of Christian friendship were woven through her life, and never more than after her diagnosis, as her health deteriorated. Benedetta depended upon her friends, and they depended upon her. They took turns holding the lamp for one another.

This story unfolds in the letters Benedetta exchanged with friends and even strangers. She was a prolific correspondent, despite her condition. She had a particular interest in lost and wayward souls. Her mother spent painstaking hours signing into Benedetta's palm the content of the missives that Benedetta received, and then served as scribe for her replies. These letters are a remarkable legacy of support and encouragement, both given and received. As Benedetta's capacities narrowed, the effects of her holiness expanded.

Benedetta had become acquainted with Maria Grazia early in medical school. At first Maria thought Benedetta standoffish and even haughty—until she discovered that Benedetta was deaf. They learned to communicate: Maria replied to Benedetta's questions in writing, handing the answers to Benedetta to read. The two became close, and their friendship is keenly evident in their correspondence over the years and in Maria's testimony at the opening of Benedetta's cause.

In a letter to Maria in 1958, one year after her diagnosis, Benedetta wrote, "Excuse me for letting off steam, but the sweetest thing about friendship is baring one's soul, isn't it? I needed to unburden mine with someone who understands."[47] And in another letter, she wrote, "Darkness is terrible, and yet I know that I am not alone: in my silence, in my desert as I walk, he is here, he smiles, he walks before me; he encourages me to bring him a tiny bit of love."[48]

Maria completed her medical training and became a missionary physician in South America. She wrote an extraordinary testimony to Benedetta's example not long before her friend's death. Her words give us a glimpse into the influence and reach of Benedetta's still, quiet life:

I will never again be alone with my fears, because you have taught me the value of prayer. You have been the way for me, you have given me proof of the existence of God. I never believed those who spoke to me of him. But it is impossible for me not to believe you who have suffered with him.

Benedetta, you have won! . . .

Not one of us is alone; you are right, we are all united in charity, one with the other. I believe in hope now.

This is all I wanted to tell you: the Lord couldn't have given you a more beautiful life, a richer one. You are so important to all of us; for me, you are the most beautiful and the dearest thing that I possess. You are the very face of hope. I am most fond of you! You are near me all the time because I am unable to separate myself from you; you are in me as a flame, as a sign.[49]

In the same way that Christ rewrites the notion of perseverance for us, so too his example renews and refreshes our understanding of true Christian friendship based on intimacy with God. Benedetta felt this intimacy more than most, and it was an experience she was keen to share with her friends and family.

She wrote to her cousin Sofia in September 1963:

All I want, Sofia, is to do what God expects of me, because everything is grace, everything is good and everything is for the glory of God. I am in peace, I am well. But if I should become afraid, I will say without shame, "Lord, I am afraid of the dark," and he will answer, "Fear not, I have overcome the world." Even Our Lady was afraid when the angel appeared to her. . . . Don't let us give up; we must never, never be overwhelmed by doubt. And if we happened to [be], just for a moment . . . he would look at us and would be able to bring us out of the tomb, alive again, like Lazarus. Holy, holy, God of hosts. Fear not.[50]

And on January 9, 1964—just two weeks before her death—Benedetta wrote to her friend Francina:

Francina, I have told you, haven't I, that I love Our Lord very much? I make the words of the psalm mine: "The Lord is my Shepherd, I shall want for nothing."

How I love the Lord, Francina darling! He who has always watched over me. And each time that I invoked him he came to my aid. Blessed be his holy name, Alleluia! Isn't it wonderful to have a Father in heaven who helps us and loves us more than we love ourselves, and who knows even the number of hairs on our head!

Ever humble, Benedetta closed the letter this way: "Francina, never tire of doing good; it is wonderful to be able to do good, and O how I wish that I could."[51]

One of her most moving letters, however, was written to a stranger, a young man who endured suffering that was similar to hers. Benedetta wrote:

Because I'm deaf and blind, things have become complicated for me. Nevertheless, in my Calvary, I do not lack hope. I know that at the end of the road, Jesus is waiting for me. First in my armchair, and now in my bed, where I now stay, I have found a wisdom greater than that of men—I have discovered that God exists, that He is love, faithfulness, joy, certitude, to the end of the ages. My days are not easy. They are hard, but sweet because Jesus is with me, with my sufferings, and he gives me his sweetness in my loneliness and light in the darkness. He smiles at me and accepts my collaboration.[52]

On January 21, 1964, sensing that her death was near, Benedetta made her Confession and received Communion. The next night, she asked her nurse to remain close by because Satan was tempting her. She said, "Emilia, tomorrow I will die. I feel very ill."[53]

In the morning, Benedetta asked her mother to read to her the "Act of Oblation to Merciful Love" from St. Thérèse, the Little Flower. As her mother painstakingly signed the prayer into her daughter's palm, a little bird landed on the windowsill. Her mother passed the bird on to Benedetta, who began to sing "Wandering Little Swallow."

The little bird flew out the window and landed on a nearby rosebush. Benedetta's mother watched as, almost instantaneously, a white rose blossomed beneath it. A rose in bloom in January in northern Italy!

She announced her discovery to Benedetta, who replied, "This is the sign I was waiting for!" She had had a dream on the previous All Saints' Day, in which she went into the family burial vault and saw it decorated with a white rose dazzling with light.

Benedetta died shortly thereafter, at the age of twenty-seven. Her last words were "Thank you."

Holding Jesus in the Palm of Her Hand

Benedetta's life is a powerful example of the graced ability to continue giving one's heart. It attests as well to the mysterious ways that Jesus helps us flourish in the most unexpected environments and to the ways by which he helps us become who we are meant to be, which is often what we most desire. Benedetta's life is also a living testimony to the profound role that Christian friendship can play in this flourishing.

The very thing that debilitated Benedetta was the thing that led to her freedom. Her suffering was the means through which she made strong, influential connections with those around her. Her life teaches us that the path to being made new in Christ is not painless, perfectly rosy, or easy.

It's not that she never experienced interior agony or even anger at this disease that robbed her of a medical profession. But in accepting her limitations, she became a doctor of another sort, a kind of surgeon to the soul. In the end, she was no less a doctor, no less a healer than she had wanted to be. Her life had shrunk, in a way, to the palm of her hand, to be no bigger than a Communion host. And yet her life was powerful and transformative, especially to her friends. She was indeed a spiritual doctor.

It is impossible to miss the correlation between Benedetta's life and Jesus in the Blessed Sacrament. He too is hidden and small, silent and even weak, but an ever-present friend to us. In getting to know Benedetta, I kept recalling this description of the Eucharist from Carlo Carretto:

In the Eucharist Jesus is immobilized. . . . He is reduced to a little piece of white bread. The world needs him so much and yet he doesn't speak. Men need him so much and he doesn't move!

The Eucharist is the silence of God, the weakness of God. To reduce himself to bread while the world is so noisy, so agitated, so confused. . . .

And yet this powerless Jesus, nailed down and annihilated, is the God of the Impossible, Alpha and Omega, the beginning and the end. As John describes him in the Apocalypse:

A judge with integrity, a warrior for justice. His eyes were flames of fire, and his head was crowned with many coronets; the name written on him was known only to himself, his cloak was soaked in blood. He is known by the name, the Word of God, . . . the King of kings and the Lord of lords.[54]

You might take Carretto's meditation into Adoration with you sometime, and with Benedetta's intercession, ask yourself, *Is this the God I meet in the Blessed Sacrament?* The beginning and the end, the God of the impossible, King of Kings with eyes of flame, a warrior for justice, his cloak soaked in blood? Is this the Holy One I encounter in Adoration?

Is this the One I approach in the Holy Mass? Is this the Mighty One I prepare to meet, to receive into my very self in the gift of his precious Body and Blood? Is my life a witness to this encounter with the Beloved, who lived and died for me? Do I recognize that this is the One who has the power to make me effective through his grace no matter my worldly condition, no matter my limitations?

Benedetta knew this God Almighty. He lived in the palm of her hand, a hand she would extend to those around her, an open hand that modeled heroically the ways she continued to give her heart to the Lord and the ways she remained present to her friends and family. She gave herself to a great Love, and that Love gave her the ability to look through death and to give us all a glimpse of the extraordinary means heaven will use to bring us to bloom.

Blessed Benedetta's witness is particularly pertinent in our day that so values the life of the body over the life of the soul. She serves in a special way as a model and affirmation for single working women, for those who suffer from progressive illnesses, for the blind and deaf, and for those in need of a friend.

Benedetta was beatified by Pope Francis on September 14, 2019.

Blessed Benedetta, your world became as small as a Communion wafer. You were immobilized, deaf, and blind, and yet you were a powerful witness to the love of God and the Blessed Mother. Jesus in the Blessed Sacrament is hidden and small too—silent, immobilized, and even weak—and still all powerful, ever present to us.

Please pray for me, Benedetta, that I will collaborate with Jesus as you did, in whatever way he wishes to use me. May I be granted the grace to allow the Almighty Father to speak through my littleness and loneliness too, for the glory of God and the salvation of souls. Amen.

IN HER OWN WORDS

I want to say to those who are suffering, to the sick, that if we are humble and docile, the Lord will do great things in us.[55]

My days are long and tiring but at the same time sweet and filled with the light of God. I strive in my exile not to lose my serenity. I recall the shouts of the Apostles when Jesus was walking on the water and said, "It is I, be not afraid."[56]

Sometimes I find myself defeated under the weight of this heavy cross. Then, I call upon Jesus and lovingly cast myself at His feet; He kindly permits me to rest my head on His lap. Do you understand . . . the ecstatic joy of those moments?[57]

FOR JOURNALING

1. What does Fr. Wickham suggest is necessary in order to persevere? A fidelity to what? And why is that important?
2. How did Blessed Benedetta embody perseverance? What were some of the effects of this profound perseverance in Benedetta's life?
3. Is there an area of your life where you struggle to persevere, where you find it hard to continue giving your heart to the Lord? Talk to him about this.
4. Do you have a friend who really makes herself present to you, someone who holds the lamp for you? Does she know how much you appreciate her? Can you let her know in a note or letter, as Benedetta did with her friends?
5. How did Benedetta's friends help make her who she was? What stands out to you about her friendships?

FOR PRAYER

Asking for the grace of perseverance, pray with

1. **Genesis 29:15-30:** They seemed to him but a few days.
2. **Psalm 111:1-10:** Great are the works of the Lord.
3. **Sirach 11:14-28:** One becomes rich through diligence.
4. **Luke 18:1-8:** This widow keeps bothering me.
5. **Romans 8:18-30:** Creation waits with eager longing.
6. **Hebrews 6:11-20:** Show the same diligence to the end.

7. **James 1:2-8:** Consider it nothing but joy.
8. **Revelation 3:7-13:** You have kept my word of patient endurance.

Asking for the grace to grow in Christian friendship, pray with

1. **Exodus 3:7-12:** I have heard their cry.
2. **Hosea 6:1-3:** He will bind us up.
3. **Ruth 1:6-22:** Where you go I will go.
4. **Philippians 1:3-11:** "I hold you in my heart."
5. **Romans 5:1-11:** While we were still sinners
6. **John 15:9-17:** "Abide in my love."
7. **John 20:11-18:** Mary stood weeping outside the tomb.
8. **Acts 4:32-35:** One heart and soul.

3

BLESSED

Elizabetta Canori Mora

1774–1825

Patience

My husband is a great student of history and, in particular, World War II. If we watch a movie or documentary about the war, he can regale me with minute details about battles and armory, strategy and leadership. It was he who told me about the poem "Wait for Me," well known to those who study the Second World War.

Its author, Konstantin Simonov, was a war correspondent from Russia. He wrote the poem for the woman who later became his wife, Valentina Serova, when he was sent to the front in 1941.

If you have seen any footage from the Eastern Front in World War II, you know that the devastation was unspeakable.

Because of the size of this theater of war and the ferocity of the
battles that raged there, the Eastern Front has been called the
largest military confrontation in history. There was staggering
loss of life through combat, starvation, sickness, massacres, and
exposure. Orders to the Eastern Front were ominous indeed.

In light of this, Simonov wrote his poem to his beloved. One
English translation goes as follows:

Wait for me and I'll come back!
Wait with all your might!
Wait when dreary yellow rains
Tell you nothing's right;
Wait when snow is falling fast;
Wait when summer's hot;
When no one waits for other men
And all the past's forgot!
Wait when those that wait with you
Are bored and tired and glum,
And when it seems, from far away,
No letters ever come!
Wait for me and I'll come back!
Wait in patience yet
When they tell you off by heart
That you should forget;
And when my mother and my son
Give up on me at last
And friends sit sadly round the fire
And talk about the past
And drink a bitter glass of wine
In memory of me—

Wait! No rush to drink with them!
Tell them to wait and see!
    Wait for me and I'll come back,
Escaping every fate!
"Just a lot of luck!" they'll say,
Those that didn't wait.
They will never understand
How, amidst the strife,
By your waiting for me, dear,
You had saved my life!
Only you and I will know
How you got me through!
Simply—you knew how to wait!
No one else but you![58]

Russian soldiers often memorized the poem, and many wrapped a copy of it around a picture of their beloved or a lock of her hair, carrying it as a kind of talisman to assure their safe return home.

Indeed, the poem does capture the power of patience, in this case through the act of waiting for the return of the beloved. It was a power that was literally life-giving. "By your waiting for me . . . / You had saved my life." That is, patience is not only something that I can practice; it is a gift that I can give. As the author Romano Guardini wrote, "The power under whose protection life can unfold is patience."[59]

We cannot overstate it: patience is a powerful force for healing, conversion, and the abundant release of grace. When practiced well—not as a kind of dull passivity but as a companion to acceptance and courage—patience will naturally lead to a deeper, richer life, certainly not one lived on the surface. The roots of the life of the patient person run deep. As a result, a patient life has a unique capacity to unleash creativity for problem solving. Fr. Wickham is helpful here:

> Since human life is so often plagued with adversity, patience is the virtue which enables us to endure it without abandoning our choice of a meaningful life. It shows us how to bend, perhaps, without ever breaking. Beyond all reason and contrary to most of the advice received, a patient person manages somehow to carry on. . . .
>
> What has given patience a bad name, however, is the notion that it mainly calls for passive submission. But this virtue must never be taken as an excuse for inaction. True patience must be closely allied with courage and perseverance, with the determination to take practical steps, to seek assistance wherever it might be found and even to invent new solutions never attempted before.[60]

Romano Guardini wrote in a similar vein:

> Patience without strength is mere passivity, dull acceptance, growing accustomed to being a mere thing. Love, too, belongs to true patience—love of life. For living things grow slowly, take their time, and have many ways and turns. Life demands confidence, and only love can trust. He who does not love life has no patience with it.[61]

For Konstantin and Valentina, neither patience nor love won the day. Konstantin eventually left Valentina, who was rumored to have had an affair while Konstantin was at war. Later she became an alcoholic, and she would die alone. But their story does not change the reality that Konstantin's poem taps into: namely, that patience, especially when practiced to a heroic level, is so restorative that it can virtually bring someone back from the dead.

Blessed Elizabetta Canori Mora practiced patience to just such a degree, and the unlikely man she brought back from the dead was her own unfaithful and abusive husband, Cristoforo.

A Note of Clarification

In the preface to the original publication of Blessed Elizabetta's life, the anonymous author wrote, "The shelter of the home and the privacy of domestic life frequently conceal the most poignant sorrows. Wives are specially called upon to suffer in secret."[62] A more modern mind might recoil from such a notion—the secret, suffering wife—as sexist poison from another era.

To avoid any possible confusion in this case, we must go straight for the jugular: Elizabetta was a victim of spousal abuse on multiple levels, including her husband's flagrant infidelities and his violent threats to her life. In our day, Elizabetta would be advised to seek counseling or a women's shelter, where she could find guidance on what steps to take and protection from her abuser. But there were no such interventions in her time, and so it seems God provided a different and more radical kind of shelter.

The Lord protected Elizabetta by taking her into a mystical world where his own presence was so overwhelming and healing that it sustained her through the protracted infidelities and abuses of her earthly husband. Because of this, she was able to raise, educate, and care for her daughters, serve the poor and estranged around her, and remain faithful in her love of the Lord.

It's reasonable to wonder, when discussing the life of Blessed Elizabetta, if the Church is somehow advocating that an abused spouse stay put and pray more novenas. We can answer clearly and emphatically: no.[63] The Church holds Elizabetta up as an example of heroic patience and charity, especially in regard to her abusive husband, but does not intend to recommend that someone remain in a dangerous, abusive relationship.

In short: If you are in danger, tell someone, call the police, flee. If your children are in danger, you have a duty to protect them. Remember Fr. Wickham's definition: "True patience must be closely allied with courage and perseverance, with the determination to *take practical steps*, to *seek assistance wherever it might be found* and even to *invent new solutions* never attempted before" (emphasis mine). In the face of cruelty and injustice, it is necessary to act.

However, you can also trust in the powerful intercession of Blessed Elizabetta to help you. There are few more powerful intercessors than those who have walked a similar road ahead of us. It's true that God sustained her partly by means of ecstasies, miracles, and mystical encounters, but he will protect and sustain you too in ways appropriate to your situation, including visceral and practical ways. Don't hesitate to ask for help—from heaven and from your local authorities.

The Powerful Arms of Patience

Elizabetta was born in Rome in 1774 to a wealthy and well-established family. She was educated by the Augustinian nuns in Cascia, and her early religious fervor led some to imagine she might have a vocation to religious life, something Elizabetta wanted to pursue. When she was twelve, she believed the Lord was asking her to make a vow of virginity, and she immediately, happily consented. She contracted tuberculosis, however, and the convent would not receive her.

Elizabetta returned home to recuperate, but as her body recovered, her soul fell into a period of religious tepidity. Rome was certainly more distracting in its worldliness than the convent, and Elizabetta, who was attracted to beauty and beautiful things, was rather caught up in it.

But God seems to claim some souls so early and with such an unmistakable hand that worldliness can never win out. Elizabetta's tepidity didn't last long, and she returned to the practice of her faith with even more fervor. Soon she received a powerful vision of the Lord, the first of many that would mark her life as more mystical than earthly. The Lord said to her:

> My child, I have seated myself at the door of your heart, so as to defend it from the entrance of evil passions. I have commanded my angels to shed over your soul a precious liquor, which has the effect of communicating to you a supernatural

simplicity to preserve you from evil and to render you inaccessible to the corruption of others.[64]

Indeed, the Father had staked his claim on Elizabetta's life and soul, and despite the extraordinary suffering she endured, she would not be torn from his hand.

Some of the "corruption" of which the Lord spoke occurred within her family. They fell into poverty because of the ill-conceived speculations of Elizabetta's self-centered and immature brothers. Then, at age twenty-one, Elizabetta met and married a promising young lawyer, Cristoforo Mora, a man of some property and privilege. For a brief time, it seemed that Elizabetta's family had been rescued from their destitution. She moved into the luxurious Vespignani Palace and delighted in the accoutrements of a life of wealth and security.

But the marriage quickly took a cruel turn. Cristoforo became outrageously jealous of the attention others paid to the lovely young Elizabetta. Eventually he wouldn't allow her to communicate with her own family, insisting she stay in the house, essentially locking her in.

At first this confinement was painful for Elizabetta, but she practiced a spirit of acceptance, an important ingredient for growing in patience. Guardini writes of acceptance as a virtue in this way: "We are not dealing with a weak submissiveness, but with seeing the truth and taking one's stand upon it."[65] Elizabetta may not have had many options, but in accepting the reality of her situation, she eventually turned her isolation into an opportunity for prayer and meditation. She found there inner peace and an ever-deepening intimacy with God.

She would need it. Cristoforo was cruel and unpredictable. One day he decided to "play" with a pistol in Elizabetta's presence. He "pretended to fire so as to amuse himself with her fright." She knew the pistol was loaded and begged him to stop, knowing that the gun could go off—which it did.

> At this moment, a mysterious voice said to him, "Stop! Stop!" and at the same time an invisible hand violently turned the direction of the shot; the ball struck against a picture representing Our Lord upon the cross, and broke the glass in a thousand pieces, leaving the image intact.[66]

Cristoforo was badly shaken by the experience, but he didn't give up his cruelties. The frightening incident cemented Elizabetta's trust in the Lord's protection. When she thought of the event later, she would break down in tears of gratitude.

Not long after this, Elizabetta gave birth, and Cristoforo was, for a short time, so delighted with his son that he seemed to forget his jealousy. But little by little, his affections soured, and he took up a mistress, upon whom he lavished so much time, attention, and money that his family was left in need.

Around this time, Cristoforo's two sisters, who were quite fond of Elizabetta, came to stay. Their company helped sustain her in the face of the humiliation and injustice of Cristoforo's very public misbehavior. Their support also helped her endure the recriminations of his family, who blamed Elizabetta for Cristoforo's behavior, suggesting she was "too retired." They didn't know that Cristoforo himself had imposed her confinement. The pain of these early years was exacerbated by the deaths of Elizabetta's first two children soon after they were born.

At one point, Cristoforo exiled Elizabetta from the palace, forcing her to live in a little apartment over the home of Dr. Mora, his father. Elizabetta welcomed the solitude, as it gave her more time to pray. When her brother came to study medicine with Dr. Mora, she gained another ally and support. And her two remaining children, Mary and Lucina, were her greatest source of joy at this time.

Not long after Lucina's birth, Elizabetta fell gravely ill with a fever that was sweeping through Rome. Her condition was so serious that she received last rites. But then, suddenly, the illness began to retreat. Elizabetta called it a miracle. She continued convalescing for five months, during which time her confessor visited her frequently.

Elizabetta later recounted to one of her daughters: "He led me to consider that the life which Our Lord had miraculously restored was no longer mine, but his. The words of his minister touched my heart. I offered myself entirely to Our Lord."[67]

Thereafter Elizabetta went to Confession at least once a week and received the Blessed Sacrament as often as possible. She cast off the fine garments that she had loved and chose to live in greater austerity and humility, a choice that some around her ridiculed bitterly. Ironically, it was Cristoforo alone, at least for the time being, who left her to live as she wished.

Meanwhile the harsh critiques of her friends and family made Elizabetta question her new lifestyle, but she wasn't left alone with her doubts. Her biographer captures this remarkable visit from a divine friend:

On the morning of the 7th of September, 1803, whilst [Elizabetta was] suffering from doubt and uncertainty regarding her new way of life, the Queen of Compassion appeared to her, holding in her hands and caressing in her bosom a dove, from which issued on all sides rays of light, and which bore under its wings marks of bleeding nails. One of these rays struck the heart of Elizabetta and made so severe a wound that she fainted away. When she recovered, she found herself completely changed; her heart was on fire, and in the excess of her transport she exclaimed, "At last, thou hast conquered, O holy love of my God!"[68]

She suffered strong heart palpitations as a result of the wound and worried that someone might notice. She asked the Lord to keep the palpitations hidden, and he did. She only experienced them after receiving Communion or during prayer. Elizabetta's life had officially entered the realm of the mystical, and she spent more and more time in that strange and beautiful world that inhabits the gap between heaven and earth.

The lives of many mystics are marked by misunderstanding and drama, and Elizabetta's experience was no different. She continued to suffer attacks on her character, and her husband continued to make public and depraved choices. He even threated her life once again.

Cristoforo stole a large sum of money from his father. Dr. Mora, overwrought about the theft, suffered a severe stroke. The Moras had Cristoforo "confined" to a religious order as punishment. At that time, the area was part of the Papal States, under the direct rule of the pope, and such confinement was a legally recognized form of punishment. The hope was that this remedy would allow Cristoforo time to pray and reflect on the error of his ways. Instead he grew furious and returned to his family wild with rage.

Though Elizabetta had nothing to do with her husband's confinement, he threatened her once again, this time with a knife. But before he could deliver the death blow, he was paralyzed with fear and lost all of his strength. Elizabetta, miraculously, was spared once again. Years later she said, "My heart was incapable of fear. Being always absorbed in God, I enjoyed an ineffable union with him. My husband might have torn me into a thousand pieces, I should not have felt it."[69]

Keep in mind that Elizabetta was called to a particular kind of sacrificial life, one in which she was even able to protect her daughters from hating their father. People encouraged her to leave Cristoforo, but in prayer it was clear to her that she was to stay with him for the sake of his salvation and for her daughters. (One of her daughters eventually became a nun and was the main scribe at Elizabetta's side, recording her thoughts and reflections later in life.) She was under the care of a number of worthy spiritual directors and was immediately obedient to them when they asked her to pray about leaving her husband. She didn't live in isolation or secrecy with respect to his abuse.

Still, as her biographer writes, "the powerful arms which served her, after prayer and the practices of penance, were silence, humility, and unalterable patience."[70] Hers was a call from God that she willingly, lovingly accepted and then was given the grace to carry out. Though we may stand incredulous at her choice, it was not an example of codependency, mental illness, or personal weakness—any more than was

Christ's choice to go to the cross—but a very particular and graced, heroic patience that measured everything against eternity. And in the mysterious economy of God, it would bear extraordinary fruit.

The rest of Elizabetta's life was marked by ecstasies, which might last days, and frequent mystical visits following the reception of the Blessed Sacrament—from Jesus as well as the Blessed Mother, St. Ignatius of Loyola, and many other saints. In several Good Friday visions, she was allowed the extraordinary privilege of accompanying Jesus in his agony in the garden and, at one time, on his way to Calvary. Angels would sometimes appear and carry her off to celestial places filled with glorious light. She practiced many mortifications, including refusing to drink anything from the evening of Friday to midday on Saturday, "in honor of the sacred thirst of Jesus on the cross."[71]

A local businessman stepped forward after being prompted in prayer to see to the care of the Mora daughters and provide for their needs. Elizabetta was given an artistic rendering of Jesus of Nazareth, an image that was later invoked in a number of miracles. She received the image as confirmation that the Lord had established himself as her Father and master. She and her daughters prayed before it every day for the rest of her life.

Many miracles attended her, especially with respect to the poor. She was so distressed at the sight of them that she would open her coin purse and give everything she had, only to discover that more coins had found their way into her purse. The same miracle of abundance took place with foodstuffs when she cooked for the poor—the bread, oil, and vegetables all multiplying to feed those she tended.

Many came to understand the power of her prayer and sought her intercession. She received prophetic words on many occasions, all of which proved true with astonishing accuracy. None were more compelling than the prophetic insight she had regarding the conversion of Cristoforo.

She Knew How to Wait

And so we return to our poem. The lover begs the beloved to wait for him, to remain faithful, to bring him back safely—even from the clutches of doom—by the power of her patience. Written during a time of war, it seems even more fitting that it should tell something of Elizabetta's life: she clearly lived out a spiritual war every day of her troubled marriage. And the power of her patience brought the soul of Cristoforo back to life through a slow, steady, credible conversion, one she predicted with great confidence and joy.

Some women friends came to visit and pray before the miraculous image of Jesus of Nazareth, and they fell into conversation with Cristoforo before they left. He chided them for their visit. "You come to pray!" he scoffed. "It is always Christmas night with my wife; but I allow her to keep it; for my own part, I say Mass whilst I am sleeping in bed."[72]

Elizabetta replied, "Laugh as much as you please, but after my death you will say Mass, and what is more, you will hear confessions. You will then no longer pretend to say Mass in bed!" The very notion of Cristoforo converting, much less becoming a priest, must have sounded ludicrous to everyone. Yet so it came to pass.

In the spring of 1825, following several bouts with various illnesses, Elizabetta died peacefully, attended by her faithful and loving daughters. With the very moment of her passing, miracles began erupting all over Rome. She appeared to her sister Mary, for example, and asked that she look after her daughters. Mary, who had been kneeling for her evening prayers, was not in the habit of having visions. Confounded by this one, she told herself it had been her imagination. It wasn't until the next day, when she visited Elizabetta's home, that she realized Elizabetta had appeared to her at the exact moment she died.

Again, at the moment of her death, Elizabetta visited a little girl who was sick in bed and waiting for her mother to bring her some supper. Elizabetta appeared resplendent in glory and announced that she was going to heaven, but she wanted to remind the little girl about a sin she had forgotten to confess. She also told her she would lead a long and holy life. The little girl's mother disbelieved the tale until the next day, when she learned that Elizabetta had perished at that very moment.

Elizabetta also appeared to a number of her friends, encouraging them in lives of holiness and assuring them of her prayers from heaven. Miracles occurred in the days following her death: the sick who approached her coffin were cured, and stunning conversions came to the hardest hearts. Healings and conversions continued to be attributed to Elizabetta's intercession as the years went on.

Certainly she was storming heaven on behalf of her wayward husband. Not long after Elizabetta died, Cristoforo began

attending Mass and took up a penitential life. According to
reports, he said often and with tears in his eyes: "I sanctified
my dear and holy wife by my bad conduct. Can I ever forgive myself?"

After some years, Cristoforo visited his daughter, then an
Oblate of St. Philip Neri, at her convent and told her that he
wanted to enter religious life. He became a Third Order Franciscan, and after some years, he was ordained to the priesthood.
Having been well educated, he served not only as a confessor
but as a professor as well. He found his greatest happiness
when offering Mass at his daughter's convent and having the
privilege of giving her Holy Communion.

Cristoforo died in 1845 after eleven years in religious life.
Witnesses testify that his conversion was sincere. He spent his
life after Elizabetta's death in penance and humility, attributing
the forgiveness of his sinful past to her intercession.

Elizabetta was beatified by Pope John Paul II in Rome in
1994, the Year of the Family. In the homily at her beatification Mass, he said:

> Elizabeth Canori Mora, amidst a great many marital difficul-
> ties, showed total fidelity to the commitment she had made
> in the sacrament of marriage, and to the responsibility stem-
> ming from it. Constant in prayer and in her heroic dedication
> to her family, she was able to rear her children as Christians
> and succeeded in converting her husband. . . .
>
> . . . *[W]e would like to pay homage to all brave mothers* who
> dedicate themselves to their own family without reserve, who
> suffer in giving birth to their children and who are ready to

make any effort, to face any sacrifice, in order to pass on to them the best of themselves.[73]

Elizabetta's remains are interred in the beautiful Roman church San Carlo alle Quattro Fontane.

Blessed Elizabetta, pray for us. Help us always to remember that patience is not so much something we practice as a gift we give. When we are tempted to give up, especially on those for whom conversion has not yet come to pass, pray for us, that we will be strengthened by your courage and heroic patience to be generous in extending this gift with kindness, always measuring our circumstances against the horizon of heaven. Amen.

IN HER OWN WORDS

Faith gives me the knowledge of the Almighty Works of God; Hope gives me an entire confidence in the Sovereign Good; And Charity makes me love God with all the strength and all the powers of my poor heart. [74]

The following is a little manifesto that Elizabetta wrote for herself:
I will keep myself unceasingly in the presence of God. I will not allow myself to be irritated by any injury or affront, however painful it may be to human nature; I will receive all with submission and joy from the hand of Our Lord.

I will never desire any good or advantage, but that which is spiritual; and conform myself solely to the Divine Will.

I will exercise myself in the practices of mortification, of penance, of humility, meekness, patience, longanimity, love of suffering, and deprivation of all which may please or flatter the senses.

I will take care not to place my confidence in any human aid; I will rely only on the merits of Our Lord Jesus Christ, and the pure bounty of Our Lord.

I desire that every breath that I draw may be an act of love of God, and of sorrow for having offended Him; and as so many acts of offering of myself to all kinds of sacrifice and suffering and even death itself, to bear witness to my love, and obtain the conversion of all those who have the misfortune not to know Him.

I will exercise myself in all theological and moral virtues; I will foster a great desire to be humiliated and oppressed. I will endeavor to rejoice amid insults and unjust reproaches. I will make a determination to die entirely to myself so as to live only the life of Jesus Crucified; henceforth I will seek only the Cross, the thorns and the nails."[75]

FOR JOURNALING

1. After reading about Blessed Elizabetta's life, are you thinking about patience in a new way? Name some specific examples.
2. How did Elizabetta embody patience? Did her patience make her more powerful? In what ways?

3. Is there an area of your life where you struggle to be patient? Is there a situation that you are struggling to accept? Talk to the Lord about this, and ask him what the gift of patience would do for the recipient in your situation. Consider that the recipient might be you.

FOR PRAYER

Asking for the grace of patience, pray with

1. **Genesis 21:9-21:** I will make a nation of him.
2. **Psalm 42:1-11:** When shall I come and behold the face of God?
3. **Isaiah 40:21-31:** The Lord renews our strength.
4. **Micah 7:7-20:** I will wait for the God of my salvation.
5. **Luke 12:35-40:** Be dressed for action.
6. **James 5:7-11:** Be patient, beloved.
7. **Ephesians 6:10-18:** Be strong in the Lord.
8. **Revelation 1:9-20:** We share our distress and endurance in Jesus.

SERVANT OF GOD

Catherine de Hueck Doherty
1896–1985

Silence

My husband and I recently bought a modest little house in a working-class neighborhood. The previous owners must have been especially fond of television; when we moved in, nearly every room, including the master bedroom, was decorated with the brackets necessary to hold a sizable flat-screen. When we first toured the house, I noticed that the television in their living room was the largest home television I'd ever seen. It loomed dark and somewhat ominous over the entire room, dominating the space like some terrible black cyclops.

The first thing my husband did after we moved in was to remove all the TV brackets that had been left behind. He couldn't stand looking at them. We put them in a box and decided to give them away. When I advertised them on a free recycling website, I got replies within sixty seconds of the post—maybe sooner. Even after I took the post down, my e-mail was barraged with replies to the tune of "I'd be delighted to take those off your hands!" A phrase I once heard kept popping into my head: "Television is the devil's monstrance."

I consider myself one of the luckiest of brides in that my husband shares my distaste for television. We have a little one, on which we watch movies and documentaries that we check out from the local library, but I haven't paid for cable in decades.

I first gave up television when I was in graduate school, studying writing. A "TV apostle" learned that I didn't have one and, aghast, showed up at my apartment one night with a huge, old monster of a TV. He walked it right into my study as though he were entering the barren desert with a lifetime supply of cold, clear water. I could see he felt positively heroic. Though it was exactly what I did not want, I didn't have the heart to refuse him, and eventually—because I lack virtue!—it found its way on, and on too often.

I gave up my television a second time some years later, in my late twenties—again, not because I'm virtuous but much more the opposite: I had the thing on *all the time*. It was the commercials as much as anything that were the real irritant. I had no idea how much they were polluting my mind and spirit until I got rid of the TV. And after two weeks of withdrawal, I knew I never wanted the thing back in my life.

What that TV was killing, and I didn't even know it, was the practice of silence. Almost the minute I got rid of it, my writing and prayer began to flourish in noticeable new ways.

I started publishing, and editors were soon seeking me out for assignments. I started not just to desire but to *need*—in a deep, almost inexpressible way—the silence of the Blessed Sacrament, where Jesus chooses not to speak. It's not that he is not able to speak through the Eucharist, but he chooses to remain silent. How very curious—a distinction I'll elaborate on in a moment.

Often when those seeking spiritual direction land in my office, they will lament not being able to pray because their minds are aswirl: "My thoughts just won't stop racing." It is a common complaint and one that Romano Guardini described more fully as "the inner turmoil, the whirl of thought, the drive of desire, the restlessness and worries of the mind, the burden of care, the wall of dullness or whatever it may be which fills our interior world as the rubble fills an abandoned well." Does this describe your last holy hour?

But Guardini goes on to say, "We must be serious about this. A life properly lived includes practice in silence."[76]

I'll often ask directees to take a media inventory: How much time do you spend watching television or on social media or on the internet? How often is your radio on in the car or at home?

They almost always say, "Oh, not *that* much." But after a few weeks of cataloguing the time—really paying attention to where they pay attention—they are often shocked at how the hours add up. They see how much energy their devices steal from them each day, as they give themselves over to things that are of little to no importance at best and positively evil at worst. Precious time, never to return.

I'll suggest to them a regimen of reading material about silence and the science behind what the internet and social media actually do to the human brain. (I'm happy to share the list!) If they need any further convincing that their life lacks enough silence, I find Guardini's chapter on silence to be the final nail in the coffin I hope they are building for their television sets. He writes: "To be capable of silence is a virtue. He who does not know how to keep silence does the same thing with his life as a man who would wish only to exhale and not inhale. . . . The man who is never silent dissipates his humanity."[77]

Indeed, Jesus never blogged, and he didn't have a website or a television. He never surfed the internet or posted on his social media account. (Imagine: "Here I am on the Sea of Galilee with my bros! #thetwelve.") In fact, none of the saints or thinkers or theologians or artists that I truly admire did these things.

Pope John Paul II came to visit the United States in the nineties. I've never been able to find a source for this anecdote, but I distinctly recall listening to the news and hearing that the pope asked his hosts, after they showed him many of the advanced technologies available in our country, "But where are your poets?" The poets no doubt died of malnutrition and are now buried under a heap of old television sets that are not decomposing in some junkyard and where, coincidentally, we also buried a good number of virtues.

Silence is a vital means to our flourishing as a civilization. It is necessary to our humanity; even Jesus needed it and sought it. He practiced it, remarkably and heroically, on a number of striking occasions. As Guardini suggests, silence is the great, desperate inhale the soul of our society needs, and needs soon, lest we fall into complete, irretrievable dissipation.

But how is silence a virtue? When we say it—"the practice of silence" or "the prayer of silence"—what exactly do we mean? Is it simply finding a quiet place to sit and zone out? Or invoking a social media fast on Sundays? Do I have to be a mystic, a contemplative, to practice silence properly? Is silence simply the absence of noise or a passive kind of emptying, like pulling the plug on the bathtub and letting the dirty water drain out?

Guardini writes, "Only he who can speak can be silent. Silence means that he who would 'go forth' by speaking remains in inner reserve; it is a knowing, a feeling, a living stillness, a vibrating from within."[78] I like to think of silence as spiritual poise, a waiting on the Lord.

Only a human being, created in God's image and likeness, is capable of silence. A rock isn't properly silent, because it cannot speak; only human beings can remain silent in a proper sense, because they have the capacity to speak, to communicate their interiority, and to choose not to.

We think of Jesus before Pilate; St. Joseph, who is "unheard" throughout the Gospel; a friend who keeps a confidence; a priest and his commitment in the confessional. Guardini adds the notion of avoiding idle chatter, "How many superfluous things we say in the course of a day!"[79] These choices are fed by silence. The prayer of silence begets the practiced poise of silence.

Of course, that's only part of it. The practice of silence will lead to a strengthening of our humanity; it will lead to greater discernment, deeper peace, and freedom of soul. Cardinal Sarah said that silence leads to "encounter, wonder, and kneeling before God."[80] It orders us interiorly. Ultimately the practice of silence increases our capacity for awe, our capacity to worship the only thing worth worshipping: the God of all creation.

We have countless examples in the Church of those who were spiritual geniuses in the practice of silence, and thankfully, many of them wrote down their thoughts about this essential habit. We are swimming in resources on how to practice and reclaim this virtue, and we ignore them at our peril.

I'd like to examine in greater detail the practice of silence in the work of Catherine de Hueck Doherty. Her writings are extremely accessible, perhaps in part because her life was so human and she didn't suffer fools unless they were fools for God. She fought the dissipation of her humanity against extraordinary odds; her practice of silence was a primary weapon in this interior battle for holiness.

Let's pay attention.

The Silence of a Lover

With a life as colorful and uncommon as Doherty's, it is difficult to know where to begin. She was a spectacular swirl of paradox: a baroness who begged;[81] an internationally recognized speaker who practiced profound silence; a divorcee who remarried and whose second husband became a priest. She lived quite literally all over the world and yet came most alive in her *poustinia*, her interior desert.

We sometimes speak of saints choosing us, deciding even to adopt us from heaven. They seem to show up in frequent and undeniable ways in our lives to point us in the right direction. For Catherine, St. Francis of Assisi was chief among the saints who must have chosen her.

Catherine likely encountered the saint of poverty as a young child, living in Egypt with her family. She was enrolled in a school there run by the Sisters of Sion. Though at the time her family was Orthodox, she was always steeped in, to borrow Pope John Paul's phrase from his encyclical *Ut Unum Sint,* "the two lungs of the Church." And Francis, it seems, a saint of the Western or Latin tradition, couldn't have cared less about Catherine's Eastern roots.

She recalled a moment when she embraced his statue, declaring, "I will be like you. I will be very poor, and the birds will eat out of my hands. And if anybody gives me bread, I will share it with the first poor child I see on the road."[82]

It was a posture that would dominate her life. This fervor for the poor and forgotten would accompany her through her flight from Russia, her escape from an abusive marriage, all the way into the poverty of Harlem, and back into the Russian *poustinik* tradition—a life of silence, prayer, and fasting—which she helped revive throughout the very noisy twentieth century.

Perhaps it was the grave difficulties of her life that drove Catherine to the interior hermitage, where in silence she met the abiding presence of God. In just the first third of her life, she experienced more than many people do in a lifetime.

Born into an aristocratic family in Russia in 1896, she lived in Egypt because of her father's work there. She married at sixteen, served on the front lines as a nurse in World War I, and was decorated for bravery. Back in Russia with her husband after the war, she was shot in the hand amid the political and social upheaval following the Bolshevik coup of October 1917. Not much later, she and her husband were present at Mass when, during the Consecration, the priest was shot. They fled the country, first to Finland, then to England, and then to Canada.

After the abusive marriage ended, Catherine lived in poverty in Harlem, working menial jobs until she was "discovered" by an agent for the Chautauqua speaking circuit. As a lecturer, she achieved financial stability. Along the way—in 1919—the baroness, "the B" to those who loved her, was received into the Roman Catholic Church and later became a Third Order Franciscan, taking a vow of poverty. All this by the time she was thirty years old.

In spite of her apostolates, writing, and speaking throughout the continent, Catherine's life was marked by controversy, misunderstanding, rejection, and a profound loneliness. All of this she embraced as a share in Christ's suffering. She even argued that we need our loneliness because of the ways it can form us. She wrote:

> You have to penetrate the mystery of Christ becoming man, and then you will know what loneliness is. It will frighten you and you will try to run from it, but stay. Keep moving into the mystery. As you move in, as the door of love, the door of obedience, the door of surrender, and the door of passionate loving opens, something will happen to you. Your loneliness will completely change.[83]

That is, our loneliness puts us in touch with the deep lone-liness that Christ experienced on earth, especially on the cross, and the longing he has for relationship with all of humanity. It is a longing he has for *you*. This was a conclusion Cather-ine reached in her practice of silent prayer.

This deeply personal encounter with Christ was something that permeated the ministries she launched, in particular Friend-ship House and later Madonna House. They were meant as refuges for the whole person, for whomever showed up at their doors. They would serve and celebrate, albeit very simply, the eternal reflection of Christ that each unique person was.

Doherty described Madonna House as a house of hospitality, "where people are received, not according to their education, not according to how wonderful they are as painters or what-ever else they can do. They are received simply as people."[84] The members of Madonna House served in very practical ways, from feeding the poor to confronting racism, from pro-viding a hot cup of coffee to providing a quiet place to pray.

As with many ministries, Doherty's efforts were sometimes thwarted or challenged. Friendship House, in particular, was beset with struggling factions and differing visions. Many at Friendship House were uncomfortable with Catherine's sec-ond marriage to the journalist Eddie Doherty. Both were free to marry in the Church; Catherine's first marriage had been annulled. Nevertheless, their marriage was met with some dis-illusion from those closest to Catherine.

The Dohertys eventually left Friendship House and estab-lished the similarly run Madonna House. In another unusual twist, the couple took vows of celibacy, and a decade later, Eddie Doherty received Holy Orders in the Melkite Rite.

Despite such an unusual path, Catherine's work led to her meeting such luminaries as Dorothy Day, Pope Pius XII, and Pope John Paul II. She influenced a generation of young people in search of God in the silence, including Thomas Merton.

Perhaps it isn't ironic that those who live lives of spectacular service—reaching into the darkest, most forgotten corners of the earth—are also men and women steeped in silence. Think of the St. John Paul IIs and St. Teresa of Kolkatas—the never tiring, incredibly productive, and wildly efficacious saints. Catherine was one of these, and it is impossible to miss the correlation between her life of silence and her exceptionally generous life of ministry. Despite the whirlwind of setbacks and obstacles in her life—enough to disorient the steadiest among us—she found a way to practice and advocate for an interior stillness before the Word of God, not as an activity but as a life posture. She wrote:

All this standing still can be done in the midst of the outward noise of daily living and the duties of state in life. For it will bring order into the soul, God's order, and God's order will bring tranquility, his own tranquility. And it will bring silence.

It will bring the silence of a lover listening with all his being to heartbeats of his beloved. The silence of a bride, who in utter joy listens to her heart reechoing every word of the beloved. The silence of a mother, so deep and inward, that in it she listens with her whole being to the voice of her children playing in a nearby yard, cognizant without effort of the slightest change in each voice. Hers is a listening silence which takes place while she competently, efficiently and lovingly attends to her daily duties.

This silence will come and take possession of lover, bride, mother, worker, nurse, apostle, priest, nun—if only the face of their soul, in the midst of their daily occupations, is turned to God.[85]

Catherine's silence was the silence of a lover. It was a passionate, consuming silence that burned like a lonely, brilliant star in the heavens and surely directed many on the road to a deeper relationship with the Lord.

Reviving *Poustinia*

Though she spent the bulk of her adult life on the North American continent, Catherine's heart was always in Russia. In particular, it was rooted in the Russian tradition of *poustinia*. The tradition isn't easily grasped in a few sentences, but generally speaking, a *poustinik* was like a hermit and yet something more.

The word *poustinia* means "desert" in Russian, and it carries something of the spirit of the Desert Fathers of early Christianity, who abandoned the world to live in the silence and isolation of desolate places. Doherty writes, "To a Russian . . . the word can mean a quiet, lonely place that people wish to enter to find God who dwells within them. It can also mean truly isolated places to which specially called people go as hermits to seek God in solitude, silence, and prayer."[86]

The *poustinik* may have lived as a hermit, but if he did, it was to make him ever more available to serve others. "A hermit of this type," writes Doherty, "went into the poustinia *for others*. He offered himself as a holocaust, a victim for others."[87]

A *poustinik* might spend several weeks in solitude and silence, only to spend the next weeks helping local farmers bring in the harvest. A *poustinik* practiced silence in order to make himself available to the world around him with freedom and detachment. The *poustinia*, often an extremely modest house where the *poustinik* lived, never had locks on the doors. Anyone was welcome at any time—to come for advice or a meal, for companionship, or to ask for any kind of help.

If silence was crucial to the lives of the *poustinikki*, of equal import was one single book: the Bible. And it seemed to be one of the most important vehicles for entering into this passionate silence. Doherty writes:

Into the poustinia the poustiniks brought one book only—the Bible. They read it on their knees, impervious to, or even perhaps uninterested in, any purely academic question. To them the Bible was the incarnation of the Word and they felt a lifetime wasn't enough in which to read it. Every time they opened it they believed with a tremendously deep faith that they were face to face with the Word.

Yes, the poustinik reads the Bible on his knees. He doesn't read with his head . . . but the intelligence of the poustinik is in his heart. The words of the Bible are like honey on his tongue. He reads them in deep faith. He doesn't analyze them. He reads them and allows them to stay in his heart . . . like Mary did. He lets them take root in his heart and waits for God to come and explain them which he inevitably will do when he finds such deep and complete faith.

When Mary was greeted by the angel she didn't totally understand what the greeting meant or what the result would be. She simply said *fiat*, "Yes." Neither did she understand what Christ said to her in the temple after three days of looking for him. Yet, she "put all his words into her heart" and that is what a Russian poustinik will do too. He will put them there and keep silent, waiting for God to take those words out of his heart and reveal to him what those words mean.

Thus the poustinik learns to know God. Not learn about him, but learn of God himself through God himself. For in the tremendous silence into which a poustinik enters, God reveals himself to those who wait for that revelation and who don't try to "tear at the hem of a mystery" forcing disclosure.[88]

Make no mistake, there was nothing weak or passive in the silence of which Catherine spoke. And apparently, to meet her, you would know this quickly, without question. Confirming this are a few stories from her life that those who knew her are fond of retelling. David Meconi, SJ, writes:

Once as Catherine approached the podium to address a seminary of pious young men, she stopped, took out her cigarette, lit up and in her throaty Russian accent began, "Okay boys, let's talk about the spiritual life." On a more serious note, she was sitting at table one evening at Madonna House when a young priest stopped in. . . . During supper he began to explain how he was off to study psychology because that is where people really needed help. "Psychology, not theology," was what people today needed. . . . [Catherine looked] him straight in the eye, and rather unceremoniously [responded], "Horse shit!" "I beg your pardon" he stammered. She continued, "You heard me. It's all horse shit. If I want advice about law I go to a lawyer. If I want help with my health, I go to a doctor. If I want to know about God, I go to a priest." Then she stared him straight in the eye and said, "Give us God!"[89]

If anyone had earned a few moments of earthiness, it was Catherine. There must be some upside to being shot by a Bolshevik.

The point stands: the singularity of the Bible in the life of the *poustinik* should teach those of us just learning to embrace the prayer of silence that we do not need to enter it alone. Rather, we take God's Word with us and allow him to speak. Our silence creates room for the voice of the Lord to be learned, to be heard, and to be heeded.

A Silent Heart Is a Loving Heart

Any life of prayer, meditation, and contemplation does not stop with the consolations one may find in her "prayer chair." Rather, the life of prayer leads to a life of action, and it orders the actions that one takes. Catherine's life was ordered toward the recognition of the absolute sanctity of a person's soul and the reverence that soul was due. Hospitality, then, was one of the great fruits of her prayer life and the work of the houses that she opened.

She once wrote, "A silent heart is a loving heart and a loving heart is a hospice to the world."[90] Her heart, her writing, and her life remain places where the weary can come and rest.

Catherine died December 14, 1985. Her cause for canonization was opened in 2000.

Dearest Catherine, do pray for us, that we may enter into the kind of silence that heals the brokenhearted.

IN HER OWN WORDS

You are about to have a rendezvous, a date with Christ. For
24 hours you are going to be alone with God and the only
book you read is the Bible. Don't take any others! If you want
to sleep, sleep. If you want to walk, walk. It's up to you. Once
you enter the poustinia, you do what the Spirit tells you to do.
There's nothing to be anxious about.[91]

True silence is the search of man for God. True silence is a
suspension bridge that a soul in love with God builds to cross
the dark, frightening gullies of his own mind, the strange chasms
of temptation, the depthless precipices of its own fears that
impede its way to God.

True silence is the speech of lovers. For only love knows its beauty, completeness and utter joy. True silence is a garden enclosed, where alone the soul can meet its God. It is a sealed fountain that he alone can unseal to slacken the soul's infinite thirst for him.

True silence is a key to the immense and flaming heart of God. It is the beginning of a divine courtship that will end only in the immense, creative, fruitful, loving silence of final union with the Beloved.

Yes, such silence is holy, a prayer beyond all prayers. True silence leads to the final prayer of the constant presence of God, to the heights of contemplation, when the soul, finally at peace, lives by the will of him whom she loves totally, utterly, and completely.

This silence, then, will break forth in a charity that over-flows in the service of the neighbor without counting the cost. It will witness to Christ anywhere, always. Availability will become delightsome and easy, for in each person the soul will see the face of her Love. Hospitality will be deep and real, for a silent heart is a loving heart, and a loving heart is a hospice to the world.[92]

The Lord from time immemorial has known you. He has allowed his fire to come down upon you like a crimson dove. His fire is over you. You are moving slowly up his mountain, the mountain of the Lord. To get to the top you must pass through the heart of God. As you pass through his heart, you become a bonfire, and together with him, a huge bonfire. You become a bonfire on the top of the mountain.

Many people see it and come to find out what it is. So they climb the mountain too; they come to your poustinias. They see that you are very strange bonfires; transparent ones. You are a bonfire through which they can pass. On the other side the heart of Christ is waiting for them. Having been yourselves scooped up by the hand of God, and having agreed to it by your yes, you have now become a transparent bonfire that leads other men to Christ.[93]

FOR JOURNALING

1. How would you benefit from practicing silence?
2. How is silence related to other virtues?
3. Take a media inventory over the next week. How many hours do you spend on activities related to social media and television? Now take a prayer and spiritual reading inventory. Compare the two inventories, and talk to God about them.
4. How might you incorporate more silence into your week? List three actions you can take to enter into a more regular practice of silence. Don't be afraid to start small. Silence has a way of expanding.

FOR PRAYER

1. **Psalm 62:1-2:** For God alone my soul waits in silence.
2. **Hosea 2:16:** I will lead her into the desert.
3. **Habakkuk 2:20:** Let all the earth keep silence.
4. **Matthew 14:23:** Jesus went up the mountain to pray.
5. **Mark 1:35:** While it was still very dark, he went to a desolate place.
6. **Isaiah 41:1:** Listen to me in silence.
7. **Sirach 20:1:** Wise enough to keep silent
8. **Isaiah 30:15:** In quietness shall be your strength.

5

SAINT

Josephine Bakhita

1869–1947

Faith and Courage

The foundational trio of faith, hope, and love are known as the theological or infused virtues—virtues that are placed in the soul, or infused, in the Sacrament of Baptism. These virtues are not exclusive to the baptized, but Baptism is the ordinary means by which they are bestowed.

It can be helpful to make a few important distinctions about how these virtues work in comparison with some of the other virtues. The *Catechism of the Catholic Church* reminds us:

The theological virtues are the foundation of Christian moral activity; they animate it and give it its special character. They inform and give life to all the moral virtues. They are *infused by God into the souls of the faithful to make them capable* of acting as his children and of meriting eternal life. They are the

LOVE LIKE A SAINT

pledge of the presence and action of the Holy Spirit in the faculties of the human being. (*Catechism* 1813, emphasis mine)

We pay special attention to this point: faith, hope, and love are *infused by God* to *make us capable* of practicing the other virtues. "The infused virtues," writes Fr. Wickham, "are *given* to each person beyond expectation and they change the very constitution of that person's being. *Faith, hope and love cannot be obtained by simply trying harder.*"[94]

This should come as good news for those of us who struggle with one of these virtues. It's not a matter of striving with greater gusto, like the hard-working engine in the children's classic *The Little Engine That Could*. We are not little spiritual engines, clenching our fists and declaring, "I will believe! I will hope! I will love!" These virtues are gifts that God bestows, imbues, infuses through the sacraments. And they can grow to maturity through our life experiences and especially in moments of conversion.

We want to cooperate with them, to nurture them as with any other virtue, but we also want to position ourselves properly in relationship to them: they are gifts, gifts we need to pray for daily, gifts our Father in heaven is delighted to give, gifts that endow us with the ability to practice other virtues. Like the father of the paralytic boy who comes to Jesus seeking healing for his son, we pray, "I do believe, help my unbelief!" (Mark 9:24).

And clearly, faith is one of the most important virtues to cultivate. Our culture suffers a scorching drought of faith. On the other hand, it often places its faith in the wrong things.

Believers must serve as credible witnesses against this absence and misplacement. As Pope Benedict wrote, "The believer should be a countervailing force against the powers that suppress the truth, against this wall of prejudice that blocks our view of God. Faith that is just beginning ought as it were to be able to lean on that kind of person."[95] He offers us the experience of the early Church as evidence of this:

> The conversion of the ancient world to Christianity was not the result of any planned activity on the part of the Church but the fruit of the proof of the faith as it became visible in the life of Christians and of the community of the Church.[96]

And so we arrive at questions worth considering: Is my faith visible? Is my faith made visible in other virtues, like courage? How do I know?

You may have tremendous faith in God, just not in the idea that God is good. You may have faith in a vengeful God or in an indifferent God, who doesn't bother himself with you. It may be that you are not lacking faith at all, but rather your faith needs refinement.

How would you describe God? Would you argue that God is good and that he counts the hairs of your head? The truth is that he is deeply interested in the details of your life and desires that you share in the goodness of his love and creation. Do you believe it?

Long before she even met Jesus, it seems that Josephine Bakhita did.

A Shattered Little Heart

Kidnapped by Arab slave traders when she was just a child, Josephine didn't know her birth date, her birth name, or the language her parents and siblings, including a twin sister, spoke. The woman who would come to be known and loved as the "little brown mother" was sold on four separate occasions and beaten almost daily during her years as a slave. Yet the woman who grew out of this terrorizing and inhumane regime later remarked, "My entire life has been a gift from God." And again, "The Lord has been good to me my whole life." And, "The Lord has always watched over me."[97]

A life of great faith often seems full of contradiction—it appears incongruous with the facts at hand. Josephine Bakhita's life bears this out. Her story—which she shared after she was freed from her early life of slavery—is ironically a testimony of courage, faith, and ultimately freedom, including the most important kind of freedom there is, the freedom to believe.

Bakhita was born in Sudan around 1868 or 1869 to a prosperous family. Her uncle was the village chief, and her parents owned land and livestock. She had a happy childhood with siblings and friends and remembered her parents as respectful of others and nature. They were very likely animists, and while practices and rituals vary widely among those who identify as such, generally speaking, animists believe that everything has a spirit or soul. Rocks, trees, mountains, rivers and lakes, animals, all of nature, and even words or concepts must be regarded as living, as having their own life force, and therefore they must be respected.

But hanging over these early years of peace and innocence was the ominous and ever-present slave trade, conducted shamefully by both Christian and Muslim traders, among others. Traders who provided slaves to Europe and the colonies prowled West Africa, but in the East, where Josephine grew up, traders supplied slaves mostly to Egypt and the Middle East.

Slave traders were known to plunder whole villages—stealing men, women, and children to be sold at auctions. When Josephine was only five or six, traders captured her eldest sister. Distraught and brokenhearted, her father searched endlessly for her, but the family never saw or heard from her again. Such episodes were all too common at this time in Sudan.

Bakhita was enjoying a normal day of play with a friend when she was stolen. As the girls were gathering herbs, two armed strangers approached them. The men tricked the girls into separating, telling the friend that they wanted Bakhita to retrieve a bundle for them in the woods and that she would meet her later, down the road. Bakhita recalled the moment:

> I did not suspect anything. I quickly went and obeyed, as I always did with my mother.
>
> As soon as I entered the woods, looking for the bundle that I could not find, I realized that those two were right behind me. One grabbed me roughly with one hand while he pulled out a big knife from his belt with the other. He put the point of the knife against my side and with a demanding voice said, "If you scream, you're dead. Now move it. Follow us." The other one pushed me, aiming the barrel of his gun at my back. I was petrified. With eyes wide-open and trembling from head

to toe, I tried to yell but a lump in my throat prevented me. I was unable to speak or cry.

Violently pushed through the thick woods, along hidden pathways and over fields, I was made to walk at a fast pace until evening. I was dead tired. My feet and legs were bleeding from stepping on sharp rocks and from walking through thorny brambles. All I could do the whole time was sob, but those hard hearts felt no pity. . . .

All I could think about was my family. I called for my mommy and daddy with indescribable anguish. But nobody could hear me there. What was worse, those two ordered me to be quiet with terrible threats.[98]

Bakhita was locked in a shed with no bed and no covering of any kind. She was imprisoned there for about a month.

"How much I suffered in that place cannot be put into words," she recalled. "I was overcome by a feeling of discouragement that seemed to shatter my heart."[99] Indeed, little Bakhita, who was only about eight at the time, would never see her family or her home again.

As with most who were stolen from the East into slavery, Bakhita was forbidden to speak her own language and forced to learn Arabic. It was her captors who cruelly gave her the name *Bakhita*, which means "lucky." She soon joined others who had been kidnapped—traveling in large caravans, herded like animals, headed to the slave markets in the north. "This is how the caravan was arranged," said Bakhita:

First the men, then the women. Everyone had a thick chain fastened around his neck, locked with a key and padlock, connecting two or three in a row. Woe to anyone who bent over or stopped—the poor necks of that person and his companion. You could see big, deep wounds around all the necks. It was so pitiful.[100]

The strongest men were forced to carry the heavy loads, the whole caravan marching long into the evening, only to be shackled by their ankles at night.

In a moment of extraordinary bravery, Bakhita and another young girl seized an opportunity to escape, spending a night in the woods evading wild beasts. It was a short-lived flash of freedom though. They were recaptured shortly thereafter by a man who tricked the girls and sold them back to slave traders.

When the caravan reached the capital city of Khartoum, Bakhita was sold to a rich slave trader. She worked in his home, attending to his daughters. That family sold her to a Turkish general. Throughout this period, her owners beat her daily for no discernible reason; at times the beatings were so fierce that it took her more than a month to recover. Slaves who became ill were literally thrown onto the manure heap and left for dead. Those who survived were treated with staggering cruelty, including the monstrous ritual of tattooing.

A woman who specialized in this ritual performed the tattooing on Bakhita and other young slaves. Bakhita remembered the woman tracing marks with white powder on the body of the first girl.

Once the marks were all made, the woman took the razor, and down it went, cutting each and every mark that had been traced.

The poor slave moaned as the blood dripped down from every wound. Once that operation was completed, [the woman] took the salt and began rubbing it hard into each wound, so that it would enter inside the cut, making it large in order for the slits to remain open. What agony, what torment! . . .

After the first victim was carried off to bed, it was my turn. . . . The woman, having been told to spare my face, began to make six cuts on my breasts and up to sixty on my stomach. Then forty-eight on my right arm. . . . [I]t seemed I was dying at every moment. . . . The scars are still with me. I can honestly say that the reason I did not die was that the Lord miraculously destined me for better things.[101]

The years that followed were marked by torturous monotony, beatings, shocking cruelties, unending labor, and constant fear. However, there was one particular torment that Bakhita miraculously escaped. Young female slaves were often raped and forced into prostitution. Many years later Bakhita told a close confidant, "I have been in the middle of mud, but I never got dirty,"[102] the implication being that she'd been spared this degradation.

Five years passed, and in 1882, Bakhita was sold one final time. An Italian consul stationed in Sudan, Calisto Legnani, bought her. He and his household would treat Bakhita with dignity. Legnani was fond of her, and he never beat or punished her.

Two years later, Legnani was called to return to Italy. For reasons even Bakhita could not understand, she begged permission to make the long journey to this strange new world with him, asserting herself in a way she had never done before. Legnani granted her request.

Hidden Mystery, New Master

Over the next few years, Bakhita's life became a tumble of fresh experiences, new relationships, and work in an entirely unfamiliar culture, climate, and geography. There was another language to learn. It was a radically new existence.

During this period, she met Legnani's friends Augusto Michieli and his wife, Lady Turina, who was a Russian and, for all intents and purposes, an atheist. When Legnani was called to return to Sudan, Lady Turina persuaded him to allow Bakhita to stay in Italy and work for her as a housemaid.

Though she was still considered a slave by the Michielis, Bakhita was put in charge of Lady Turina's daughter, Mimmina, and served as her nanny. The bond of affection between them was sincere and mutual. Bakhita gained the complete trust of the Michielis, so much so that when her mistress made the decision to return for a year to Suakin where her husband was running a hotel, she was confident leaving her daughter in Bakhita's care. Mimmina was not yet three years old and the long trip would have been difficult for one so young.

During this period, Bakhita met a spiritual patron of sorts, Illuminato Chechinni. He was the estate manager for the Michielis and a hero to the local peasants and the poor because of his advocacy on their behalf. A man of deep faith, he was also the first human being since her enslavement to take a personal interest in Bakhita and, in particular, her religious formation.

He gave Bakhita her first crucifix, a moment she recalled many years later with tenderness and wonder:

> As he gave me the crucifix he kissed it with devotion, then explained that Jesus Christ, the Son of God, had died for me. I did not know what a crucifix was, but I was moved by a mysterious power to keep it hidden, out of fear that [Lady Turina] would take it away. I had never hidden anything before, because I had never been attached to anything. I remember that I looked at it in secret and felt something inside me that I could not explain.[103]

This was her introduction to the *Paròn*, an intimate and affectionate title that Bakhita would give to her heavenly Father. In the Italian dialect she had learned, it means "master."

Considering that Lady Turina would be away for so long, Chechinni recommended that she place Bakhita and Mimmina in the care of the Canossian Sisters who ran the Institute for Catechumens in Venice.

Lady Turina at first resisted the idea, but she was convinced by Chechinni, especially after he signed a promissory note that he would cover their tuition if for some reason Lady Turina was ever unable to pay it. The Canossian Sisters received Bakhita and Mimmina with genuine warmth, and before long they were both being catechized in the Catholic faith.

And it was there that Bakhita, so long refused the fullness of her personhood, began to see herself as a welcome member of an unlikely and beautiful family. Roberto Italo Zanini, in his exquisite and insightful biography of Bakhita, describes her first year there:

For the first time since she was made a slave, she felt completely at peace and found emotional and spiritual comfort. And this was due not only to the human warmth and profound openness of [Sr. Fabretti, her tutor]. It was the gradual discovery of her own spiritual and mystical dispositions that steadily filled her with joy.

It was at the Institute of Catechumens that the young African woman began in a prayerful dialogue to become family with the Paròn and with Our Lady, both of whom, step by step, came to take the place of father and mother in the "orphan's" life. It was here that the long periods of meditation began: before Christ Crucified, before the tabernacle, before the Madonna's image.[104]

It was a burgeoning relationship that would soon be tested, even to the highest courts in Italy.

Conversion and *Coraggio*

For some, like St. Paul, conversion comes with being knocked to the ground. God breaks in dramatically and makes himself known with a violent but necessary jolt to the soul. For others, like Bakhita, conversion is a quiet, gentle gathering of a richer vocabulary with which they can express a truth they already seem to know. Like a low flame, conversion grows in strength and intensity, radiance, heat, and purity.

Even as a young girl in Africa, Bakhita had a strong sense of the divine. She recalled, "In the morning I watched as the sun was born and in the evening as it set. And I thought that if it was beautiful, how much more beautiful must be the one who had made it."[105]

There were other moments when she felt the presence of the divine breaking undeniably into her life. She couldn't have articulated it at the time, but she later revealed that her guardian angel had guided her during the night she spent in the woods evading wild beasts. And there was the remarkable fact that her purity had been preserved even in slavery, something she credited entirely to God.

Despite her inability to write or to read, Bakhita proved to be a receptive and eager catechumen. As the months passed, she came to understand her *Paròn* in a much more personal way. Her curiosity and wonder over Chechinni's devotion began to take on a life of its own within her, and she grew in firm determination to be baptized in the Catholic faith.

Everything in her new environment supported this. Even the room she shared with Mimmina cooperated in her conversion. The cupola of the Basilica of Santa Maria della Salute (Our Lady of Salvation) completely dominated the view from their window. The basilica had been erected to honor the Blessed Mother for having quashed the bubonic plague of 1630. This plague took the lives of almost one-third of Venice's residents, and Our Lady's help prompted all of Venice to turn to her in times of need. This history very likely influenced Bakhita's earliest understanding of Mary as a powerful intercessor and spiritual mother.

And there was more. Inside the basilica was a Byzantine icon of Madonna and child. "It is an image before which Bakhita probably stopped and prayed before she took Mimmina out on walks during free time," suggests Zanini. "A black Madonna, as is frequently the case in Byzantine iconography, the Madonna della Salute bears in her arms a little black Jesus. Just like Bakhita."[106]

It was as if the world around her was inviting Bakhita into a new identity—to claim her place as a beloved daughter of God and to find an eternal family from which she would never be separated and who supported her in the strong yet gentle arms of freedom. Bakhita recalled of this precious time:

> Those holy mothers instructed me with heroic patience and introduced me to that God who from childhood I had felt in my heart without knowing who he was. I remembered [as a child in her village in Africa] looking at the moon and stars and the beautiful things in nature and saying to myself, "Who is master of all these beautiful things?" And I experienced a great desire to see him and know him and honor him.[107]

It was a desire whose fulfillment would be seriously threatened. After nearly a year, Lady Turina returned to Venice to finish up family business, retrieve her daughter and Bakhita, and go back to Suakin, where she and her husband planned to remain permanently. Bakhita was not yet ready for Baptism and didn't want to leave. Lady Turina became enraged when Bakhita informed her. Thus unfolded a battle of literally royal proportions.

Lady Turina bombarded Bakhita with all the reasons she was obligated to return to Africa; the quiet, soft-spoken Bakhita was unmoved. Lady Turina circled her wagons. She issued threats, and she returned to the Institute again and again with "reinforcements" of a wide variety, including her brother, a military officer. Bakhita remained firm. Lady Turina even consulted with the attorney general of the king, who reminded her that slavery had been abolished in Italy, and so Bakhita was free to do as she pleased.

In these difficult days, Bakhita, whose life had been marked by an obedience born of terror, spent many hours in prayer before the crucifix. "It was the Lord who filled me with such firmness," she recalled, "for he wanted to make me all his."[108] We could argue that it was a moment she was infused with faith, a faith that fed her courage.

Even as Lady Turina dragged the distraught Mimmina away from her, Bakhita, who sincerely loved the child, remained firm in her determination. "I will not leave the house of the Lord," she said. "It would mean my ruin."[109]

This was no overstatement. Bakhita understood that a return to Suakin meant serving behind the bar of the Michielis' hotel in a city that was overrun with adventurers, brothels, and debauchery.

We cannot overstate the courage it took for Bakhita to stand her ground. Even some of the nuns with whom she lived tried to convince her to go with Lady Turina, to keep the peace. Cardinal Agostini was consulted, along with the superior of the Institute and various other power brokers, each with their own say.

Throughout the kerfuffle, the quiet, obedient woman from Africa—stolen from her childhood, enslaved and beaten with the most severe cruelty, unable to read or write—had no resources and not a single possession save Chechinni's crucifix. Yet she stood firm. She would remain in Venice, she would be baptized, and she would practice her newfound Catholic faith for the rest of her long and holy life.

Fr. Romano Guardini reminds us:

> Courage means placing our hand in his and following him, in small things and in great. The way may lead us very far. We know of persons who follow it so far that they escape our comprehension; these are the saints. We hear them speak, we read their writings, but essentially they have gone beyond us, with God. This is the highest challenge.
>
> If there is a regret which is most bitter at life's end, it is this: I heard the call but did not follow it.[110]

Bakhita, a little slave named Lucky, would have no such regrets.

Forward Out of Love

We could argue that it was Bakhita's faith—with her in some way even in childhood—that helped enliven her courage in that moment. Because that is what faith, hope, and love do: they strengthen us in the other virtues because they tell us who we are; they establish our identity. Courage, in particular, must rely on them, for the courageous, in a profound way, know who they are as beloved children of God.

Fr. Wickham writes:

> The courage of Jesus . . . enabled him "to drink the cup of salvation" for others. But this courageous choice was sustained by

his marvelous reliance on the Father. He handed himself over trustingly without reservation (but not without experiencing fear, as Gethsemane reveals) despite his vivid awareness of the worst death that awaited him. This was possible because *his faith, hope and love were fully realized*.[111]

Jesus knew who he was; he knew his lineage and to whom he belonged.

Therein lies the root of all spiritual work: the robust realization of faith, hope, and love. These in turn bring about the fullness of courage—and patience, gentleness, perseverance, and so on. We have said that faith is largely, first, a gift—a gift we cooperate with and nurture. Maybe Bakhita had received a bigger dose of faith than others, and this gave her tremendous courage and resolve when she needed it most. Hers is a striking example of finding one's true identity in Christ. Once she knew who she was, a daughter of God, nothing else mattered.

"The powers of evil on earth cannot truly harm us as long as we gaze on the face of God and rely on His merciful love alone,"[112] Fr. Wickham wrote. Surely, as Bakhita gazed upon the face of Christ crucified, she must have sensed this truth. Jesus was there, witnessing to her, lending her his own faith and courage, adopting her as his own. Surely, in that black Madonna and child, Bakhita began to see herself more clearly. Everything that had been distorted through slavery and sin was illuminated by truth.

According to Fr. Wickham:

The courage of Jesus is clarified, then, in the choice he made at his climactic hour. His decision was, rather than to doubt in any way, to renew his entire confidence in the Father's fidelity. . . . In practical terms this breakthrough may recur in every exercise of Christian courage.[113]

To act with courage, then, is to act in a way that affirms our identity. We join our courage to Christ's when, even in small ways, we choose to lean into the Father's fidelity. Bakhita looked at the cross and saw courage born of faith. Then she chose to join her suffering to the suffering of Jesus. "It is in union with Christ the risen Lord that we receive the grace of courage," Fr. Wickham concluded. "Despite our fear of the evils threatening our path, we may learn how to participate in his choice to go forward out of love."[114]

Bakhita learned this way forward—through her friend, Chechinni, and her tutors, through the face of that Madonna and her baby, and through Christ crucified. She went forward out of love.

Beloved Brown Mother

A few years after her Baptism and First Communion, Bakhita discerned a call to religious life and entered the novitiate at the Canossian convent. She lived the rest of her days in the northern Italian cities of Verona and Schio. One sister who lived with her remarked that "when you were near her you understood that there was something extraordinary about her."[115] A priest who worked closely with her in the last half of her life claimed that Bakhita "lived and breathed her faith and had a sense of dignity and gentleness. . . . [E]verything she did made one think that she had reached a high level of virtue."[116] Still another priest recalled:

> It was evident that she had supernatural faith. It was enough to watch how she prayed and comported herself in church—the way she genuflected, the way she made the sign of the cross. How she smiled after every visit to the chapel. Everything pointed to a profound and intimate union with God.[117]

Children flocked to Bakhita, and she was fond of telling them stories of her life as a slave, occasionally even showing them the scars on her arms. Countless religious and priests attributed their vocations to personal encounters with her. She loved to make others laugh, even through her own clumsiness. She would occasionally break into silly dances during periods of recreation, and she loved to tell the story of a little child who thought she was black because she ate too much chocolate. She was genuine, simple, and wise, according to witnesses, and many sought her intercession.

Notably, Bakhita announced that she would forgive her captors, even to the point of thanking them. She said, "If I were to meet those slave traders who kidnapped me and those who tortured me, I would get down on my knees and kiss their hands, because if that had not happened, I would not be a Christian or religious today."[118]

Mother Josephine Bakhita died February 8, 1947. At her canonization Mass, Pope St. John Paul remarked:

[S]he came to understand the profound truth that God, and not man, is the true Master of every human being, of every human life. This experience became a source of great wisdom for this humble daughter of Africa.

In today's world, countless women continue to be victimized, even in developed modern societies. In St. Josephine Bakhita we find *a shining advocate of genuine emancipation.* The history of her life inspires not passive acceptance but the firm resolve to work effectively to free girls and women from oppression and violence, and to return them to their dignity in the full exercise of their rights.[119]

Truly a saint for our times, St. Josephine Bakhita stands in the gap of our racial discord. In the growing divide that flows from ignorance and hatred, she announces to all her faith made visible, her courage unleashed: "Freedom is only found in the love of God."[120]

Pray for us, St. Josephine Bakhita, for our thorough conversion and awareness of the dignity inherent in every human being. Help us to learn through your example, to follow the way of the cross with courage, to speak on behalf of those who cannot speak for themselves, and to fight for an end to human trafficking and racism and for the right to worship our God. May we go forward out of love as you did, St. Bakhita, with an uncompromising faith.

IN HER OWN WORDS

I give everything to the *Paròn*, and he takes care of me; he is obliged to.[121]

Be good. Love the Lord. Pray for the unfortunate ones who do not know him. Know that it is a great grace to know God![122]

FOR JOURNALING

1. Is there an area in your life where you feel enslaved? Perhaps in a behavior like addiction, shopping, or chronic negativity? Can you speak to the Lord about this and ask him to guide you to freedom?

2. Take a faith inventory. Is it strong? Weak? In need of an infusion? Is your faith visible? How?

3. Can you remember a time when your faith was unusually strong, a time when you sensed an infusion from the Holy Spirit? What happened, and how did it change you?

4. What is your spiritual identity? How would you describe yourself to a nonbeliever? How would you describe your Father?

5. How did courage and faith interact in St. Josephine's life?

6. Can you recall a time you really needed courage? What happened? Did you get the grace you needed?

FOR PRAYER

Asking for the grace of an infusion of faith, pray with

1. **Isaiah 40:9-31:** The sovereign Lord is coming.
2. **Matthew 8:5-13:** Cure of the centurion's servant
3. **John 3:11-17:** Everyone who believes will live forever.
4. **Romans 4:1-12:** Abraham's faith in God
5. **Isaiah 45:20-25:** I am the only God there is.
6. **Psalm 25:1-22:** To you, O Lord, I lift up my soul.
7. **Luke 7:11-17:** The widow of Nain
8. **John 6:60-69:** Lord, to whom would we go?

Asking for an increase in courage, pray with

1. **Judith 13:1-20:** Your trust in God will never be forgotten.
2. **Matthew 14:22-32:** "Courage! It is I!"
3. **Matthew 25:14-30:** Parable of the talents
4. **Hebrews 10:32-39:** Do not lose your courage.
5. **1 Samuel 17:41-54:** David and Goliath
6. **Psalm 56:1-13:** I trust in God and am not afraid.
7. **1 John 5:1-15:** We have courage in God's presence.
8. **2 Corinthians 3:4-12:** The power we have comes from God.

SAINT

Mary of the Cross, Mary MacKillop

1842–1909

Hope and Wisdom

We said earlier that some virtues seem to fit like two hands folded in prayer—for example, perseverance and friendship. Hope and wisdom share this same sensibility. We were created for hope—hope in eternal life—but to cultivate a vibrant theological hope, we must make friends with hope's shrewd older sister, wisdom.

Hope and wisdom take turns holding the lamp for one another; they stand shoulder to shoulder in mutual support. Both hope and wisdom are directional: they face forward and yet know what lies behind them—they are never ignorant of history. Neither are they afraid of it.

Like great faith, hope and wisdom know themselves. Wisdom keeps a hand on hope's shoulder, mindful of hope's youthful energy, always leading the way. In that mystical way by which we carry others with us, hope and wisdom together hold the *risen* Christ.

There are a few distinctions to be made. First, there is *natural* hope: "I hope the harvest is good," "I hope we elect pro-life legislators," "I hope I find good work." Hope as a *theological* virtue is something more than this. As a theological virtue, "hope," writes Josef Pieper, "is the confidently patient expectation of eternal beatitude . . . ; hope expects from God's hand the eternal life that is God himself." [123]

Seen in this way, hope is something like Google Maps for the soul: it gives you your exact, eternal destination. And— don't miss this bit—hope is both confident and patient.

Furthermore, "hope, as a virtue, is something wholly supernatural." [124] We said that faith was infused, given as a gift to be received and nurtured. Hope shares this attribute. One theologian said it like this:

> Christ is held by the hand of hope. We hold him and are held. But it is a greater good that we are held by Christ than that we hold him. For we can hold him only so long as we are held by him. [125]

And there is wisdom in the holding. Writing about the virtue of wisdom, Fr. Wickham says: "It is the Christian community which 'holds' the risen Lord in its depths and retells the story of his life." To grow in wisdom, then:

> All the members . . . need to commune "reflectively"—that is, like mirrors catching reflections from an interior Source

of light—in order to know and be more fully transformed by the wisdom of Jesus, the mystery of his teachings on the Kingdom of God.[126]

Hence our emphasis in this book on praying with Scripture. True wisdom, by this definition, means that we hold the *risen* Jesus interiorly. I think sometimes we do very well at holding the suffering Christ, but how well do we move through this world holding the risen Jesus in our depths? Measuring everything that happens against the reality of the resurrection? For that is true wisdom.

Hope and wisdom side by side can move through every kind of trial and corruption, even within the Church, not only because of the crucified Christ but because of the risen Lord. There is saintly genius in the ability to hold these two realities, indistinguishable and intermingled, in one heart.

Cross Bearer

How appropriate, in the beauty that is the universal Church, that we travel to yet another continent in search of holy women to guide us in virtue. We find in Australia the witness of St. Mary of the Cross, Mary MacKillop, the first Australian saint.[127]

Her parents had both emigrated from Scotland looking for new beginnings in a new world. Alexander MacKillop and Flora MacDonald met and married in Melbourne, Australia, a city that had been established only seven years earlier and was brimming with potential in 1840. Mary, born in Melbourne, was the MacDonalds' first child.

When Flora was pregnant with Mary, her parish priest gave her a relic of the True Cross, and Flora wore it around her neck. MacKillop's official biographer, Paul Gardiner, SJ, suggests, "This gesture was subsequently interpreted as the first consecration of the future *Mary of the Cross*."[128] Divine consecration or no, it was incredibly appropriate, as we shall soon discover.

Mary was described as a beautiful child, wise beyond her years. Despite the impoverished and rather rough world that Australia was at the time, Gardiner notes:

> Abundant evidence shows that Mary was a well-educated, well-informed woman. Her writings display, in faultless English, a strength and clarity of thought that point to some steady source of literacy and culture. . . . ; it can only have been the influence of her ex-seminarian father.[129]

Alexander had spent nearly eight years in preparation for the priesthood in Scotland and Rome before abandoning his pursuit of the presbyterate. Surely the immense task of being educated and formed for priestly life left a deep spiritual and intellectual impression on him that benefitted his family. From the time Mary was a young child, she experienced a desire to give herself completely to God; perhaps in this she was a bit like her father. She often spoke of "the debt of gratitude she owed her parents for sharing so fully with her their Catholic faith and piety."[130]

And yet Mary's early years were strained and lonely. "My life as a child was one of sorrow, my home when I had it, a most unhappy one,"[131] she said. Her father, though good hearted and well educated, was an imprudent and naïve businessman. His ill-fated ventures landed him in serious debt and sent his family of eight children into dire poverty. They moved frequently in pursuit of other hapless prospects and rarely if ever enjoyed a peaceful domestic grounding.

At sixteen, Mary went to work, first as a governess, later as an assistant in a stationery firm, and then back as a governess—all to support her family because her father was incapable of doing so. She was not relieved of that grave duty until she was twenty-five.

The sociocultural landscape in Australia was also supremely challenging, and it was sometimes a contributing factor in Mary's unhappy early life. The poorly developed road system for the vast country was dangerous and rough, and lacked drainage. Drought and forest fires occasionally devastated the predominately agrarian economy. A significant amount of anti-Catholic sentiment resulted in legislation meant to stamp out Catholic education. These realities would complicate Mary's life and those she served in incalculable ways.

Still, throughout these early years, Mary nurtured a quiet life of prayer and service, and a desire began to take shape within her. She wrote:

> I looked for a poverty more like unto that practiced in the early religious orders of the Church, a poverty which in its practice would make a kind of reparation to God for the little confidence now placed in his Divine Providence by so many of his creatures.[132]

Mary's calling as a cross bearer expressed how profoundly she lived this poverty.

Converging Hopes

It was in the tiny inland town of Penola, in southern Australia, about halfway between the port cities of Adelaide to the northwest and Melbourne to the southeast, that Mary first took work as a governess, in 1860. There she crossed paths with Fr. Julian Woods, the local priest who became her spiritual director and to whom she confided her desire for religious life.

The territory under Fr. Woods's direct pastoral care was vast, and most of the children in that area had no access to education, religious or secular. Fr. Woods hoped to open a Catholic school that anyone could attend, regardless of whether they could pay. When he met Mary, he wondered if she might be the answer to his prayers and a fulfillment of his hopes. Perhaps he could appoint her headmistress of a school that would tend to the youngest and poorest of his flock. Slowly the dream unfolded.

Mary had to move around for various jobs, in order to help her family financially, but she was finally able to return to Penola. There, with the support of Fr. Woods, she started a Catholic school in 1866. Launched in a former stable, it looked more like a mud hut than a schoolhouse, but her brother John helped renovate it so that it was usable. The only other instructors serving with Mary in these modest beginnings were three of Mary's younger sisters, two of them "willing but uncertain."

In a letter to her mother in 1866, Mary wrote, "Had it not been for the loving care of God, who sent me what then certainly appeared many sorrows, I might after that have lost the grace of my vocation. Thanks be to God for every little sorrow I had."[133] Like so many of the saints in their early formation, she was already giving thanks for her crosses, seeing them not as burdens but as gifts that would refine and strengthen her.

By 1867 other young women had joined the ranks of the MacKillop sisters, and under Mary's guidance and direction, more schools were opened. The "Josephites," Australia's first religious order, was slowly being born and, in the process, taking on additional apostolates, which included opening orphanages and homes for the elderly and girls at risk. The sisters relied entirely on providence for their support, never asking a single penny for their services and choosing to live in a poverty as severe as the poverty of those they served. The local bishop approved the rule of the Institute of St. Joseph by 1868, and the Josephite sisters began to wear a simple brown habit.

In the following years, Sr. Mary played a key role in building and expanding the institute. "The record of the distances she covered by coach, rail, and steam is hard to believe," writes Gardiner. "It took a toll on her health, which was never robust."[134] She made several trips to New Zealand, where she opened more schools, and she traveled tirelessly to visit her sisters in distant outposts as they struggled to serve the poor, uneducated, and vulnerable.

"Let not your crosses . . . make you unhappy," she told her sisters. "Look upon them as stepping-stones to an eternity of happiness, and value them as the most precious presents from a good and loving God."[135]

Mary also traveled to Rome to meet with the pope and work toward formal recognition of the institute. Getting papal approval for the Josephite rule was a significant burden on its own and fraught with strife at home and in Rome, which we will examine in more detail.

In these years, those who knew Mary and worked alongside her were always heartened by her charity, stamina, and unshakable hope in God's providence. Young sisters recalled bagged, hand-delivered meals received at the train station from a breathless Mother Mary who had realized they would be without dinner until late at night.

Sr. Mary's idea of relieving hunger among the poor wasn't limited to opening soup kitchens but included "handing over to a hungry man the actual dinner she was about to eat."[136] She traveled on third-class trains only because there wasn't a fourth class. She encouraged her sisters to travel in steerage when they traveled by boat, noting, "Our religious habit will protect us there. . . . [T]hough the world may think it a disgrace to religion to travel there, we may feel quite sure that our humble and despised God does not."[137]

The Way of the Cross

Many of Sr. Mary's letters testify to her holiness. In 1869, for example, as persecutions blossomed around her, she wrote:

> I feel a peculiar pain when I hear of a cross coming to us from the hands of a good person. I think it brings me closer to God, without ever making me think harshly of that person. I can

only see in such instruments in the hands of God for the puri-
fication of His children, and as such, persons for whom we
should pray as amongst our most powerful benefactors.[138]

She lived in an authentic way the challenging words of
Jesus in the Gospel of Matthew: "Pray for those who perse-
cute you" (5:44).

For despite the great goods that were pouring out of the
young order, Sr. Mary's vocation was marked by unusual turmoil and a regular showering of calumnies. As the bishop
drafted the rule for the order, he drifted from its original
impetus, and the rule no longer seemed to fit the austere life
of poverty that Sr. Mary desired. She wrote a respectful letter to the bishop, suggesting that perhaps she should pursue
religious life in another order. In response, the bishop ordered
her to leave Adelaide, where she'd been leading the order. She
requested a meeting with the bishop before her departure. Her
request was reported as a refusal to obey his direct order and
resulted in her "excommunication."

When the truth of the matter became known, the bishop's
censure was declared invalid, and Sr. Mary was quickly rein-
stated. She went on about her work with the same faithfulness
and cheer as ever she had possessed, without displaying the
slightest bitterness over the whole ridiculous debacle. She held
the priesthood in highest esteem and would never let her sisters utter a negative word about the priests and bishops with
whom they worked. She told them she'd rather have a dagger
through her heart than hear anyone profane the priesthood.

Over the years, an unfortunate tension also developed with Fr. Woods. Early in the life of the order, he had "alienated many of his fellow priests with his policies and his style,"[139] an alienation that he would later transfer to Sr. Mary and the institute. When she was sent to Rome with the rule to seek approval, the Holy See rewrote it, including a clause whereby the institute could own property. Sr. Mary objected, but she was overruled. Fr. Woods took this revision as a direct affront to him.

This placed Sr. Mary in a difficult position. She wanted to obey Rome, and she wanted to honor Fr. Woods. To do both was simply impossible.

Letters to friends and relatives indicate her clear awareness of the evil that was trying to thwart her. She once remarked, "My title, the happy one given to me at my profession, implies a life of crosses and afflictions."[140] She had no illusions about the cost of a holy life.

For our purposes, we will concentrate on one of the more significant trials of Sr. Mary's life, the great crusade of the 1883 Adelaide commission, in which those who opposed her work intensified their efforts to stop her. They falsely accused her of embezzling funds that should have gone to the poor, of intemperance with alcohol, and of imprudently incurring debts. Supposedly she managed all this while she traveled tirelessly over great distances, with great difficulty, in service to the poor.

The players involved in this scandal are too numerous and their machinations too complex to render in full.[141] Her accusers—these included priests, bishops, and religious—went to astounding lengths to manufacture charges. In short we will say that, under false pretenses, the bishop was induced in 1883 to compose and sign a formal document claiming to have Papal authority for a commission of enquiry into the affairs of the Josephites. In fact, the Holy See knew nothing of the affair—it had sent no document at all, not even one which the two diocesan authorities could have misinterpreted.

The Sisters of St Joseph believed that they were submitting to a Commission directly authorized by the Holy See, and during the course of the operation its Papal status was frequently brought to their attention.[142]

To make matters worse, while the "evidence" was being collected, there was no opportunity to present a defense. "There was no cross-examination, no challenging by the defense, because there was no defense. . . . [T]he accused was unaware she was being charged."[143]

As Mother Mary slowly began to realize that her honesty was in question, she would only reply, "Our good God allows us to have much opposition from some of his best servants, and to me this is a painful cross."[144] It was a cross especially cruel and devious in its delivery. Gardiner writes:

Some weeks after the bishop had assured Mother Mary that the interrogations had revealed nothing serious, and that there was much to be grateful for, she received a letter from him out of the blue full of reproach but with no mention of specific serious charges, commanding her to leave the diocese forthwith. She had, he informed her, lost the confidence of the Sisters, and no longer held any jurisdiction in his diocese. In her letter of submission she expressed surprise but no bitterness, and gave not the slightest hint of resistance.[145]

Instead she followed the instructions she was given with alacrity and professed to her sisters:

> The Institute is passing through a severe trial, but with humility, charity, and truth on the part of its members all will in the end be well. Have patience, my own loved children—pray— pray humbly and with confidence and fear nothing. Our good God is proving his work.[146]

In Christ Alone

Let us pause and rest with this for just a moment. Mother Mary wasn't naïve or simpleminded or unaware of the import of such accusations. She bore them in full, and though falsely accused, she obeyed without flying into a wild and well-earned posture of self-defense. She stood like Jesus before Pilate and trusted in the Father's plan—though it could mean the end of her and possibly her life's work.

The spiritual poise that Sr. Mary demonstrated in this event—and in countless other tests of her vocation—is simply astounding. It had to be born of a spiritual friendship with Christ on the cross, a friendship that was too deep for words. She would not abandon Jesus, she would not leave his side, even when it meant she had to climb up on the cross herself and be crucified by her own confreres. She knew who she was, in hope, and this allowed her to respond in wisdom.

Over time truth prevailed. Her "alcohol addiction" turned out to be an occasional nip of brandy before bed, as directed by a doctor. Every single debt was accounted for, including one that the bishop had approved in writing. And of course there was no embezzlement of any kind. Many statements offered by her sisters had been twisted or taken out of context to present a fallacious rendering of Mother Mary's relationship with her charges.

"The whole affair is a mystery to me," Mother Mary wrote to one of her superiors after the truth had been revealed, "but I hope God will be glorified in the end and his most holy will worked out."[147]

Mother Mary's response to the bishop's actions was equally generous. "The Bishop is really a holy, hard-working man," she wrote. "I cannot believe but that he meant all for the best, and if in saying that he acted in virtue of instructions from the Holy See he has made any mistake, I believe that he has been urged to it by others."[148]

Mother Mary's hope was never in persons, save one: the person of Christ. She was not naïve about the suffering of the human condition; she was raised in it. She had no worldly advantage that could distance her from the poor, and she never wanted one. She carried on, in spite of cruel, innumerable, and painful betrayals, because she held on to Jesus—and he clearly held her. The risen Jesus had her in the palm of his nail-scarred hand.

At her canonization, Pope Benedict XVI began his comments on St. Mary with a reference to 2 Timothy 3:14-15:

"Remember who your teachers were; from these you can learn the wisdom that leads to salvation through faith in Christ Jesus." For many years countless young people throughout

Australia have been blessed with teachers who were inspired by the courageous and saintly example of zeal, perseverance and prayer of Mother Mary MacKillop. She dedicated herself as a young woman to the education of the poor in the difficult and demanding terrain of rural Australia, inspiring other women to join her in the first women's community of religious sisters of that country. She attended to the needs of each young person entrusted to her, without regard for station or wealth, providing both intellectual and spiritual formation. Despite many challenges, her prayers to Saint Joseph and her unflagging devotion to the Sacred Heart of Jesus, to whom she dedicated her new congregation, gave this holy woman the graces needed to remain faithful to God and to the Church. Through her intercession, may her followers today continue to serve God and the Church with faith and humility![149]

And no matter what corruption may surround us, may we continue to defend—tenaciously, bravely, and at all cost—that which is holy.

St. Mary of the Cross, pray for us, that when faced with corruption and malicious attacks on our faith, we will anchor our hope in the risen Jesus, just as you did. Pray that we look upon our crosses and those who inflict them as gifts, blessings from a good and generous God. Strengthen our resolve to spend more time in God's Word, that we may become wise and credible witnesses in retelling the story of Christ's life. Amen.

IN HER OWN WORDS

If anything should grieve me, it would be the fear that any might feel disappointed at so much devotion being apparently unanswered. Let me beg that no one will think so. The prayers will all be heard—if not as we wish—as God sees best.[150]

Let not your crosses . . . make you unhappy. Look upon them as stepping-stones to an eternity of happiness, and value them as the most precious presents from a good and loving God.[151]

As far as I'm concerned in this matter, I have, thanks to the infinite goodness and mercy of my God, so firm a conviction that some day sooner or later He will confirm us in these things that I cannot say I have *one anxiety* as to the final result, indeed I sometimes wonder so much at my confidence upon this that I would think I was too sanguine or over presumptuous were it not that in my heart I know that it is in God alone I trust for the fulfilling of His promise that those who trust in Him shall never be confounded.[152]

FOR JOURNALING

1. Is there an area in your life where you feel particularly hopeless? What do you think St. Mary of the Cross might say to you about this?
2. Take a hope inventory. Is your hope strong? Weak? In need of an infusion? Where are you "located" in terms of eternity?
3. How does Fr. Wickham define wisdom, and what does this mean to you?
4. How do hope and wisdom work together?
5. Make a plan for growing in wisdom, that is, in spending more time in God's Word. Involve your whole family in this plan.

FOR PRAYER

Asking for the grace of an infusion of hope, pray with

1. **Isaiah 35:1-10:** Flowers will bloom in the desert.
2. **Psalm 27:1-14:** I will never be afraid.
3. **John 14:1-14:** "That where I am you also may be."
4. **Romans 8:31-39:** Nothing can separate us from the love of Christ.

5. **Isaiah 40:1-11:** They have suffered long enough.
6. **Psalm 42:1-11:** I will put my hope in God.
7. **Luke 12:35-40:** Be ready for whatever comes.
8. **Mark 8:22-26:** A blind man from Bethsaida is cured.

Asking for an increase in wisdom, pray with

1. **Wisdom 7:22-30:** A pure and radiant stream of glory
2. **Matthew 5:1-11:** The new Moses; the Beatitudes
3. **1 Corinthians 1:18-25:** God's foolishness is wiser than human wisdom.
4. **Colossians 2:1-10:** Hidden treasures of wisdom and knowledge
5. **Luke 2:41-52:** The boy Jesus in the Temple
6. **John 17:20-26:** The glory you gave me before the world was made
7. **1 Corinthians 3:18-23:** Become a fool to be really wise.
8. **Sirach 4:11-19:** Wisdom takes care of those who seek her.

7

SAINT

Mary Magdalene
The Time of Christ

Love

We have saved love for the end. Not because it is the least important but because it is the most important, the most fundamental. Aquinas teaches that love is the mother of all other virtues, and very often love is the most difficult, the most demanding of them.

As matriarch and ruler, love exacts forgiveness and demands reconciliation in the face of the most painful betrayals. She asks us to extend our hearts to our enemies and to pray for the conversion of our persecutors. She requires that we bring our sinfulness into the light, repent, and make amends. She asks more of the human heart than any other virtue, perhaps because she is willing to suffer the most on its behalf. Love would die to remain true to herself.

And we have saved love for the end because its loss, or its abuse or distortion, wreaks the worst havoc on the soul. We exist in a paradoxical kind of tension with love. Josef Pieper notes:

> At bottom all love is undeserved. We can neither earn it nor promote it; it is always pure gift. It is . . . "the prime gift" that makes all other gifts possible. But there seems to be in man something like an aversion for receiving gifts.[153]

Benedict XVI has written that the fear of being unloved is the greatest anxiety of all; he calls it "the horror of complete isolation."[154] So we must resolve this tension in the human heart: that we long for love and at the same time resist it, hold it at arm's length—most especially the unconditional love of God. This tension can inhibit our ability to love virtuously and to live fully.

So often the women who find their way to me for spiritual direction suffer from a crippling tension between desiring yet avoiding love. They are driven by a single fear: that they are fundamentally unlovable. Whole lives can be lost to this pernicious lie and the traumatic unrest of soul it creates. Uprooting it—and replacing it with the Truth, with Jesus—has been a common thread in the lives of many of the holiest among us.

It seems to me that this fear of being unlovable might have been a fundamental struggle for Mary Magdalene and one of the reasons for her tremendous spiritual appeal. Scripture tells us that she was possessed by seven demons; it does not describe her as a prostitute or her life as one of debauchery, notions that recent popes and Scripture scholars have been at pains to correct. As we will see later in this chapter, that depiction arose, in part, through a misreading of Scripture.

Nevertheless, we can imagine that, possessed by demons, Mary thought of herself as unlovable, a lie from which Jesus freed her when he freed her from those demons. He freed her with love so that she could accept love and live by love, even with all of love's tremendous demands. Once Mary Magdalene encountered Jesus of Nazareth, she wouldn't have it any other way. The love of God is transformational. The arc of her life resembles those of our lives, we hope: from sinner to faithful friend to saint.

Some of the traditional stories of Magdalene that have stretched across the centuries are legends, and we will look at a few of them in greater detail. But without question, her primary draw is at the tomb of Jesus, where her deep love sent her searching for him, only to discover that, once again, *he* would find *her*. That garden moment is critical, when the Lord calls her by name, and she turns to recognize him and falls at his feet, clinging to him.

How we long to do the same, to find that our greatest love is not lost after all, that the living Christ recognizes us personally and passionately, and that we cling to him in love, relief, and gratitude. We long to be that privileged one to whom he does not delay the knowledge of his living presence and the joy of his resurrection. Thus Magdalene's universal appeal.

We all falter at love; we fall down where love is concerned. But I want to assure you, it is never too late to grow in this virtue, or rather to receive it and allow it to take deep and holy root in you. Pope Benedict wrote:

It is not a headlong leap into heroism that makes someone a saint but patiently and humbly walking with Jesus, step by step. Holiness does not consist in adventurous achievements in virtue, but in joining him in loving.[155]

If love needs revision in you, a reboot, a deeper conversion, Jesus is here, calling your name, calling you to him passionately and personally. The greatest love of your life has not been lost and never will be.

Who Needs Your Love?

The Church bursts at the seams with sinners and saints who would help us find our way in love. Volumes have been written on the many shades and types of love. (Josef Pieper claims he spent twenty years writing one chapter on love alone!) But for our purposes, I want to concentrate on one simple and central love, the love of the Good Samaritan. We could call this the love that simply asks, in this moment, *where am I needed?*

Pope Benedict is especially helpful here, as he examines the well-known parable in which Jesus expounds on love of neighbor (see Luke 10:25-37). You will recall that a traveler falls prey to robbers and is left injured on the side of the road. Two respectably religious men pass by, a priest and then a Levite, neither of whom is willing to extend himself to aid the man. Only the Samaritan—a member of a group despised by the Jews—responds in love. Benedict writes:

The Samaritan comes along without any theories. His heart tells him what love is: to help the person who needs me here and now with everything I have and can do; to treat that person as if that person were myself; to love that person as myself. . . . The parable teaches us that it is not the big ideas that save the world but the courage to tackle what is at hand, the humility that follows the voice of the heart that is the voice of God.

The parable thus aims at awakening our heart so that we learn to see where our love is needed.[156]

We can take this parable as a starting point for a revealing examination of conscience, asking, how well have I offered my love when someone has needed it?

It's an especially important question to ask for the simple fact that love so often sits at the core of conversion, like that of Eve Lavallière, a star of the Paris stage in the early twentieth century. Lavallière encountered the love of Jesus in large part through reading about the life of St. Mary Magdalene and her encounter with Jesus at the tomb. She underwent a sweeping and compelling conversion, living the end of her life as a penitent—a truly happy penitent.

Eve was moved by the then widely accepted notion of Mary as a "fallen" woman, but she also embraced Mary as the beloved disciple of Jesus, the one Jesus chose to encounter him at the tomb and, perhaps more importantly, the one he sent on a mission to tell the others, "I have seen the Lord" (John 20:18).

A Modern Magdalene

Eve Lavallière was born Eugénie Maria Pascaline Feneglio on Easter Sunday, April 1, 1866, a happenstance that was almost prophetic in linking her to the Easter encounter of Mary Magdalene with the resurrected Jesus. As a child, however, Eugénie would never have imagined a connection between herself and the Mary of Easter morning. Her father, a costumier, was chronically unfaithful to his wife and a violent alcoholic prone to fits of jealous rage directed at Eugénie's mother. Throughout her childhood, Eugénie and her brother, her only sibling, witnessed numerous violent outbursts and domestic beatings. They lived in constant fear and a state of hypervigilance.

Years later Eugénie recalled one particular moment of childhood joy: her First Communion. She remembered it as the happiest moment of her life, though it seems to have quickly skipped over her like a stone skipping on the water, eventually sinking way down deep. The Eucharist is a powerful encounter, and it rested at the bottom of Eugénie's soul, hidden yet ever present. One day she would again be united with the Blessed Sacrament.

Until then, to escape the tumult of her home, Eugénie would visit a neighbor's house where she felt welcome and safe. There she began to demonstrate her talent for theater, putting on plays to relieve the stress of her family life. Her biographer Charlotte Kelly writes:

These plays and recitations gave her the only happiness she had known up to this, for they made her forget the miseries of her home life, and she lived for the time in a wonderful world of her own. As composer, stage manager, costumier and principal actor, all in one, she was the leading spirit of these little entertainments and gained whole-hearted applause.[157]

It would be an inadequate and short-lived reprieve. At age seventeen, Eugénie and her brother watched in horror as their father drew a gun on their mother and shot her. Next he pointed the gun at Eugénie, but she dodged the bullet. Finally her father turned the gun on himself, shooting himself in the head. He died instantly.

Eugénie and her brother fled the house. To make matters even more tragic, Eugénie never saw or heard from her brother again. Her mother struggled for life for two months but finally succumbed to her injury. Eugénie, officially orphaned, was sent to live with relatives, with whom she did not get along.

When she proved too unruly—she was strong-willed, rebellious toward authority, frequently brooding over the injustice of her circumstances—Eugénie was sent to an orphanage, where she fared little better. She ran away and eventually landed work in a hat shop.

Eugénie was popular and successful there, and her fashion sense earned her the nickname Eve Lavallière, after the Duchess Lavallière, a renowned fashion plate. The name stuck. Ambitious and beautiful, Eve was relieved to have a new identity, and one tied to royalty at that.

She longed for something beyond the provincial. Eugénie dreamed of a more exotic life in Paris, in the theater. One day she happened upon a poster of the then famous French actress Jeanne Granier. The image captivated her, and it must have fanned the flame of her imagination regarding life in the theater. It wasn't long before she found her way to Paris. She took singing lessons, at which she excelled, and she soon won a modest role on the stage. She was thrilled at this beginning, but she remained mostly in obscurity for the next ten years, something against which she railed interiorly. She was determined to be discovered and enjoy the security and glamour that she imagined would accompany fame.

Eugénie got her break around the turn of the century, when she was cast in a substantial role alongside none other than Jeanne Granier. Reviewers said she stole the show. It seemed the die was cast: she would be catapulted into stardom. Quick-witted, a tremendously believable actress, and inclined toward extemporaneous and unpredictable moments on stage, she soon became one of the most sought after and popular leading ladies of her time. Accolades, awards, and wealth came flooding in.

The great Sarah Bernhardt was among her champions. "What wonderful gifts you have!" she said. "What you have cannot be learnt. It must be inborn. . . . You have something of the genius in you."[158]

The genius of Eugénie attracted the powerful and prominent. The best directors fought over her; kings and queens asked to meet her. She lived in opulence on the Champs-Elysées and purchased an additional flat in a more private area, where she could rest from the adulation and increasing demands of her fans.

Over the next sixteen years, Eve lived a wild life of parties, wealth, glamour, and romances, moving from success to success.

No remnant of the terrorized, misunderstood, orphaned, and abused Eugénie remained. Eve had taken her place, and she'd made it.

As her career on the stage flourished, however, Eve's interior life grew darker and more disturbed. She became addicted to drugs. Her longtime romantic partner left his estate to Eve's only daughter, not to Eve. She indulged herself as a mistress and had multiple relationships with men who were equally unfaithful to her.[159] She knew nothing of real family life. Eve "was alone in a world that applauded the great artist, but knew and cared nothing for the woman."[160]

One evening, following a particularly well-acclaimed performance, as the thunderous applause still echoed in her mind, Eve walked to the River Seine intending to drown herself. It was not the first time that she had seriously contemplated suicide. "Even when I was at the height of my success," she recalled years later, "I used to leave the stage victim to sadness I cannot describe." At another point, she said, "A voice seemed to follow me everywhere saying, 'Eve, you weren't made for this sort of thing.'"[161]

During World War I, she willingly served many charities by giving free performances, but by May 1917, Eve was on the verge of a nervous breakdown. She had signed a contract to tour the United States in the coming year, and she knew she could not keep the commitment without a complete rest. She decided to spend several months in the French countryside before going abroad. The decision changed her life and remade her very soul.

"Exit Stage Left"

Eve departed for the western province of Touraine with only
her maid and a companion, Leona, a refugee from Brussels. She
took up residence in a beautiful, remote château that just happened to be in the care of the local parish priest, M. Chasteigner.
It was an ideal spot for rest and recuperation and a total departure from her life in Paris. She is described on one occasion as
sitting on an upside-down pail, completely enthralled as she
watched a local farmhand milk a cow.

The day after her arrival, on a Sunday afternoon, the priest
came for a visit. As they strolled around the property, Eve
regaled him with assurances of her deep satisfaction with country life. The next few scenes could only have been written and
choreographed by the Holy Spirit. Eve's biographer captures
the action this way:

> M. le Curé listened smiling, for a while; then he said quietly: "By
> the way, Mademoiselle, I did not see you at Mass this morning."
>
> Lavallière was startled. It was a long time since anyone had
> challenged her so directly.
>
> "Well, M. le Curé," she said at last, "I didn't like to come
> without your permission; after all, you know who I am—Laval-
> lière of the Varieties. Still, if you've no objection . . . "
>
> Now, the Curé knew too much of the world to be surprised
> at her absence; but she was one of his parishioners now and
> he would treat her as such. So he replied, "Objection? Why
> should I object? The church is open to everyone. Anyway I
> shall continue to expect you."

Lavallière smiled and no more was said. But the following Sunday she was at Mass, kneeling in the midst of the peasant folk. M. Chasteigner preached of great penitents, beginning with Magdalen and continuing the series each succeeding Sunday. One day, Lavallière, who was now on very friendly terms with him, ventured to say: "There is one thing you forgot to put in your sermon."

"Quite possibly," [he replied]. "What is it?"

"My name at the end; because it was certainly for my special benefit that you were preaching."[162]

When Eve left Paris, she left behind a whirl of distractions and empty aspirations that kept her in a constant state of unrest and longing. In the country, it was as though she was finally able to settle enough to hear her own soul and the Holy Spirit, who was so intent on reclaiming it.

It came to Eve's attention in the days that followed that her companion, Leona, had not received her First Communion. It wasn't long before the two were visiting M. Chasteigner daily for catechesis. During one of their visits, Eve admitted to dalliances with the occult. The priest warned her sternly about this, and the warning took hold. She began to ask herself, and with some trepidation, "If the devil exists, then why not God too?"

Her heart began to stir, wondering about the nature of her life, the possibility of God, and what this could mean for her. Seeing his charge distressed, M. Chasteigner lent her a volume on St. Mary Magdalene written twenty years earlier by Jean Baptiste Henri D. Lacordaire. He suggested she read it, prayerfully, on her knees. She did. Copious tears fell, and the woman who arose thereafter was a new creation.

Lacordaire's Magdalene

We must pause Eve's story for a moment to reflect on St. Mary Magdalene and Eve's introduction to her. Magdalene has always been a somewhat complex figure within Church history. Legends and traditions abound as to who she was, where she lived after the resurrection, and miracles attributed to her before her death.

One of the most popular panegyrics about the life of Magdalene comes from the Italian writer Jacobus de Voragine, archbishop of Genoa, around 1260. Voragine compiled what is known as *The Golden Legend*, a compendium of stories about various saints based on lore and tradition. Writing of Mary, he said:

> One day Mary Magdalene heard Jesus preaching from afar in the town of Bethany, and was moved to tears. This incredible experience immediately altered her life forever. She began waiting in the distance just to see him again and to listen to him talk to the people of Bethany. Her heavy heart overflowed with tears of bitterness at the same time as tears of joy, for she had finally discovered true Love.[163]

This was very much the Magdalene who captured the imagination of Jean Baptiste Henri D. Lacordaire in the nineteenth century. Emphasizing that great love of Jesus, he intentionally and fervently dedicated his book on the Feast of the Sacred Heart, 1880. It is available in English, but there are a number of important pages missing from the English translation—namely, those describing Magdalene's experiences at the foot of the cross and on resurrection morning.

The bulk of Lacordaire's work is an ardent account regarding why he firmly believed in the tradition that places Magdalene in France in the last years of her life—living in seclusion, simplicity, and deep prayer. This is the legend Voragine promoted in *The Golden Legend*. The story suggests that a number of Christians, including Mary Magdalene, were cast out to sea in a rudderless boat to die—this as punishment for preaching the Gospel. They miraculously landed on the southern shore of France, occupied at the time by Rome. Mary Magdalene was successful in converting the town's leadership, practicing pagans, when she prayed for the prince's barren wife, who then conceived. Mary Magdalene spent the next thirty years in solitude, living in a cave as a penitent on behalf of sinners.

It is largely this legend that moved the Frenchman Lacordaire to argue that Magdalene's relics were truly in France, in a basilica, as many claimed. He celebrates the relationship between Magdalene and the French people, noting that the Crusaders would stop at her church on their way to Jerusalem to ask her intercession in their quest. He also argues for a popular conflation of Marys: that is, that Magdalene was the woman who broke open an alabaster jar at the feet of Jesus, anointing him just before he entered into his Passion (Mark 14:3-9). He contends that she was also the woman who washed the feet of Jesus with her tears (Luke 7:37-38).

Perhaps most moving of all, Lacordaire tells of the striking friendship that existed between Mary Magdalene and Jesus, remarking:

Friendship is the most perfect of all human affections, because
it is the most unfettered, the purest, and the deepest. . . .
[F]ounded on beauty of soul, it has its source in regions freer,
purer, and deeper than those of any other feeling. [164]

His direct entreaty to the reader must have moved the heart
of Eve deeply and personally. He wrote:

Whoever you are who read these lines, if ever you have known
tears of penitence or those of love, refuse not to Mary Magdalen, who has loved and wept so much, one drop of that perfume
with which she embalmed your Saviour's feet.[165]

This combining of texts and tales probably began at least as
early as the sixth century, when Pope Saint Gregory the Great
stated in a provocative homily: "We believe that this woman
[Mary Magdalen] is Luke's female sinner, the woman John calls
Mary, and that Mary from whom Mark says seven demons
were cast out." He further suggests that "the ointment used
by Luke's unnamed sinner, now Mary Magdalen, to anoint
Christ's feet had previously been used by her 'to perfume her
flesh in forbidden acts.'"[166]

Historians point out:

It was Gregory who also associated her, again primarily through
identification with Luke's unnamed sinner, as a penitent when
he explained that by immolating herself at the feet of Jesus,
"she turned the mass of her crimes to virtues, in order to serve
God entirely in penance."[167]

There are other traditions around Magdalene. Eastern thought places her holding an egg before Caesar. When she announced that Jesus was risen, the story says, the emperor replied, "He is no more risen than the egg in your hand is red." Immediately the egg turned red.

Other accounts suggest that it was Mary of Egypt and not Mary Magdalene who ended her life in prayer in a French cave. The thought is that the two were confused over the centuries. Whatever the exact details may be, Lacordaire seems to capture the import of Mary Magdalene's essence:

No name stirs such echoes as does hers; her sinfulness awakens human sympathy, and her virtue forms a link between her and the generation of the "pure of heart." Mary Magdalen touches both sides of our life; the sinner anoints us with her tears, the saint with her tenderness; the one embalms our wounds at the feet of Christ, the other dries them at the moment of his ascension.[168]

This was certainly the Magdalene whom Eve met while on her knees.

The Leading Lady of Penitence

So moved by Lacordaire's account of Magdalene was Eve that her full contrition and confession soon followed, along with reception of the Blessed Sacrament. For the first time since her childhood, she received Holy Communion, along with Leona, on June 19, 1917. For the rest of Eve's life, she counted her age from that day.

Though her previous life was capricious, Eve's conversion was unwavering. When M. Chasteigner expected her to return to the theater, she corrected him. "Now that I know what it is to live, I can't possibly go back to that existence." And she meant it. She cancelled her future engagements and gave up her fine clothes and makeup. Eventually she gave away the lavish belongings that she had left in Paris.

Rumors began to circulate: Had she ruined her looks in some beauty treatment gone wrong? Was this all a publicity stunt? One rumor even suggested that she had become a spy and was in a German prison.

But Eve was far from a prisoner; in fact, she was probably free for the first time in her life. When a friend visited, Eve was eager to relay, "When people mention me to you, make it quite clear to them, all those who know me, that you have seen the happiest, indeed, the most perfectly happy of women."[169]

In the years that followed, Eve spent all her energy pursuing God. Her biographer writes, "She had but one desire left—to love God. 'To love, whatever state or disposition I find myself placed,' she writes: 'May the will of Jesus be my law, may His love be my life.'"[170]

Eve gave away most of her money, keeping the most meager sum to meet the needs of her household. "Love, love to give and have nothing of your own," she wrote to a friend. "Give even your generous thoughts, give your sufferings, give your merits, divest yourself of everything in order to become the dearly-beloved of Jesus, in order to gain an immortal crown."[171]

She prayed earnestly about how she should serve and made many trips to Lourdes, even living there for a time. She traveled on multiple occasions to North Africa, where she and Leona cared for the sick. She made several attempts to join the Carmelites but was refused, and eventually she became a Third Order Franciscan. It was as if the question "Where is my love needed?" had been indelibly written into every cell in her body. Whatever the answer to that question and wherever it took her, she went with complete surrender and joy. Eve was at peace.

Her fervor came at the cost of her health, a price she was happy to pay. She wrote:

> What does it matter whether I live or die? Let Him reign alone, everything lies in that! To want, to do, to love nothing but His will. . . . I want to die to the world and to myself in order that Jesus may reign alone in me.[172]

And reign he did.

Eve frequently worked herself into total exhaustion and illness. In 1924 she returned from another trip to North Africa knowing she would not make the trip again. Her ravaged body could no longer accommodate the strains of such service.

She spent her last years in Thuillières, France. She lived in utter simplicity and suffered a number of serious illnesses. She welcomed these as an opportunity to live out greater penitence and to grow in holiness. She wrote at that time, "There's a lot to be done if I am to tame this horrible nature of mine."[173] And in another letter, "I am the vilest of wretches, the most defiled, a veritable sewer, and Jesus surrounds me with His protection, in a word, loves me, and I feel His love; it is almost palpable!"[174]

Near the end of her life, Eve contracted a terrible eye disease and needed an operation. She couldn't receive anesthesia because of her history with heroin. Alas, she declared, "You and I, Jesus!" and then turned to the surgeon and told him to proceed.

The surgery failed. Eve's eyelids had to be permanently sewn shut, all without the benefit of pain medicine. It was torturous, but Eve endured it "with unbroken calm." She prayed, "Open the eyes of my soul, that I may contemplate Thee and love Thee, adorable Trinity, even if I must pay for it with the death of my bodily eyes."[175]

Eve died peacefully on July 10, 1929, as the Litany of the Blessed Virgin was being prayed at her bedside. She is buried in the humble cemetery at Thuillières. Her gravestone bears two simple lines that Eve chose herself: "I have left all for God. He alone is sufficient for me."

In Magdalene's story, Eve found something of her own: the unconditional love and mercy of Jesus and the power to love that this bestowed on the recipient. And so this modern Magdalene, who was born on Easter, was born again when Jesus made his presence known to her in that quiet French countryside, calling her by name while she prayed on her knees.

"It is only rebirth in being loved," writes Pope Benedict, "that completes birth and opens up for men and women the space of meaningful existence."[176] A meaningful existence that ever asks, where is my love needed?

St. Mary Magdalene, your great love of Jesus sent you searching for him, and instead he found you! Pray for us, that we will also search for Jesus with the eyes of our soul and rejoice when he finds us in lives of service to those who need our love. Amen.

IN HER OWN WORDS

Because we do not have many words of Mary Magdalene upon which to reflect, we will allow Eve to speak on love.

Lord God of my heart and soul, behold me. I am Yours. The flesh is weak and complains, but my soul is ready. *Fiat voluntas Tua!* Even did I wish to love something other than Thee, Lord, I could no longer do it. Anything that I might have loved is now only desolation, ruin, infamy.[177]

The world which gives its approval is made up of beings who do not know God, who live solely for the life of this earth, and think neither of their souls, nor of death, nor of hereafter: it's a world which accommodates itself to everything and doesn't care. I can't do it; my whole being revolts at the idea, and if I remain joyful and calm, the reason is that God has changed my soul, has destined it for himself, and wants to show me, before I definitely go to Him, the emptiness of everything else. I feel lonelier here than anywhere else. I am Earth's eternal orphan: all my life I have sought in vain for my heart's nourishment, that nourishment of tenderness and affection, to which my heart has always aspired and yet never attained. My heart was being starved to death, for all that it was given was truffles and champagne, and it needed plain healthy food.[178]

I have had a lot to suffer here at the hands of the third-class newspapers; there are some abominable things. I don't mind, however, for with God's good help I bore everything bravely. But even with these mud-slingings, as silly as they were cowardly, there has been much room for satisfaction. People are so full of admiration that I am confused and disturbed by it. I am leaving [show business] without a regret, without a turning of the head. I am leaving with a heart full of a sense of duty, and with a very real support from Above, and that is a joy which no one can understand, and which no one can take from me.[179]

FOR JOURNALING

1. Pope Benedict writes that we need to learn to see where our love is needed in the present moment. Who needs your love right now? How might you bestow it? Consider that the person who needs your love in this moment might be you.

2. What would it mean to you if you felt completely love-able? How would you change your life if you knew you were totally loved?

3. Lacordaire concludes his work on Magdalene: "As Mary Magdalen on the evening of the passion, so may I break the frail vase of my thoughts, and scatter them at the feet of Jesus!"[180] What tears, what thoughts, what hopes would you like to offer Jesus as an anointing?

FOR PRAYER

Through the intercession of St. Mary Magdalene, pray for a deeper love and a knowledge of where your love is needed.

1. **Deuteronomy 7:7-13:** Because God loved you
2. **Ezekiel 36:22-32:** "You will be my people."
3. **Hosea 11:1-11:** My love for you
4. **1 Thessalonians 5:12-28:** Do good to one another.
5. **Romans 13:8-10:** "Love is the fulfillment of the law."
6. **Luke 10:29-37:** Parable of the Good Samaritan
7. **Mark 14:3-9:** Anointing at Bethany
8. **John 15:12-17:** "Love one another as I love you."

Epilogue

Humility and Magnanimity

I'm the sixth of seven children—"the Magnificent Seven," as my godmother used to call us. My younger brother, Jon, number seven, was much anticipated at our house, especially by my older brother, Joe. At eleven years old, Joe was the only boy among five girls, and understandably and to everyone's amusement, he made his hope for a little brother well known.

The day after Jon was born—a boy indeed!—I made a pile of posters from construction paper with earnest proclamations of joy: "A child is born, praise the Lord!" and "Unto us a son is given!" and the like. I decorated them with the very best crayon drawings my six-year-old hands could muster and taped them up all over the house early in the morning, before anyone else was up. As my Dad was getting ready for work, he discovered some of them and, with a broad smile, started reading them aloud.

When I heard them being read, I was suddenly struck with embarrassment and ran around the house ripping them all down. I was sure that if my older siblings saw them, I'd be teased. But some little part of me, even decades later, wished I had left them up—teasing or no.

It was a moment in which my childlike heart dared to believe in greatness and beauty in the world. Though I would not have articulated it, I was celebrating how, out of love for us, God takes our littleness and invites us into his greatness. The birth of my baby brother was a perfect example of this. It was a wonderful gift to have a baby brother, and this boy in particular; he was something to celebrate. Every baby is special, of course, but to me, there was something unique about *my* baby brother. I've known it my whole life.

Many years later, at his priestly ordination, which was very near his thirty-eighth birthday, I told my brother Jon this story about pulling down his posters when he was born and how I always regretted it. So I made him a new poster. This time I used my little nephew's crayons—again with great proclamations of joy over Jon's birth and the tremendous gifts he brings to the world, the Church, and his priesthood.

How privileged I felt to be able to call my brother Father. I felt I had recovered something for my six-year-old self and for my brother. Something was made right in the universe. An awareness of our nobility as children of the Father, heirs to his kingdom, was somehow restored. How wondrous that we are part of God's creation.

Why do I tell this little story in this epilogue on humility and magnanimity?

A Thought of God

Throughout this book, we have paired some virtues because they help illuminate one another. Like the right wine with the right cheese, they bring out the flavor and goodness in the other. Humility and magnanimity are two such virtues. Josef Pieper writes:

> Humility is not primarily an attitude that pertains to the relationship of man to man: it is the attitude of man before the face of God. Humility is the knowledge and acceptance of the inexpressible distance between Creator and creature. . . .
>
> The proper impulse of natural hope . . . is toward the virtue of magnanimity. Humility is the protective barrier and restraining wall of this impulse.
>
> Magnanimity, a much-forgotten virtue, is the aspiration of the spirit to great things. . . . A person is magnanimous if he has the courage to seek what is great and becomes worthy of it. This virtue has its roots in a firm confidence in the highest possibilities of that human nature that God did "marvelously ennoble."[181]

We don't often think of humility's "sibling" as magnanimity, but Pieper names their intimate connection:

> Nothing shows the way to a correct understanding of humility so clearly as this: that humility and magnanimity not only are not mutually exclusive but also are near to one another and intimately connected; both together are in opposition to pride as well as to faintheartedness.[182]

Pieper suggests that humility—recognizing the great expanse between humanity and God—prevents magnanimity from getting too big for its britches. Humility keeps magnanimity in check. As Pieper makes plain, in order to flourish in the art of being human, we need both these virtues: humility to recognize our littleness and magnanimity to recognize our greatness. And so I suggest that we can only recover one if we also recover the other. And too often magnanimity is brushed aside, like a pesky baby brother who wants us to play with him but whom we're too busy to pay notice.

When I think of magnanimity, I'm reminded of these words of Pope Benedict XVI: "We are not some casual and meaningless product of evolution. Each of us is the result of a thought of God. Each of us is willed, each of us is loved, each of us is necessary."[183]

More than ever, we need to remember that our lives are not random accidents of biochemistry but ordained to wonder and a share in the very life of God. My little six-year-old self, making her earnest posters, recognized and claimed this and wanted to celebrate it. But as so often happens, magnanimity was shamed out of claiming its place right next to humility. The world is quick to sell us perverse ideas about what greatness is, and in the process, we can end up shunning our true nobility.

By becoming one of us, Jesus has ennobled human nature; he has made humanity holy. We must honor and celebrate this ennobling in one another, even when our brothers and sisters cannot see it. And we must serve and love our brothers and sisters in humility, even when they refuse or disdain our service and love. In short, we must hold magnanimity and humility in a delicate, dynamic balance.

We were not created to dwell in gutters and settle for filth, chaos, disorder, and ugliness. Though the expanse between humanity and God is great indeed, he reaches down and touches creation with his grace and magnificence, that we might lead lives of dignity, righteousness, beauty, meaning, and order.

You are made for nobility; you are your Father's daughter. In his marvelous little book *Humility of Heart*, Fr. Cajetan Mary da Bergamo writes:

> In Paradise there are many Saints who never gave alms on earth: their poverty justified them. There are many Saints who never mortified their bodies by fasting, or wearing hair shirts: their bodily infirmities excused them. There are many Saints too who were not virgins: their vocation was otherwise. But in Paradise there is no Saint who was not humble.[184]

And I would argue, there is no saint who is not also magnanimous, seeking what is great and striving to be made worthy of it by God.

What Is Great

This *seeking what is great* is serious business, of course, and one easily diluted, maimed, marred, and distorted. We need to be vigilant about refining our sensibility regarding what is great and what we seek: we want to seek the greatness recognized by God. This is where humility becomes essential in the pursuit of holiness.

A few years ago, I went through a period of feeling a little pinched by ambition: a little too consumed with "likes" and sales and how many folks were visiting my website or reading my column. Some of this is all right; it's good to have some enthusiasm for success in our work. But it must be managed.

My spiritual director, who does not suffer fools or vanity, declared in his straightforward manner: "Vainglory." And he quickly assigned me the Litany of Humility, written by Rafael Cardinal Merry del Val (1865–1930), to pray several times a day.

O Jesus! meek and humble of heart, **hear me.**
From the desire of being esteemed, **deliver me, Jesus.**
From the desire of being loved, . . .
From the desire of being extolled, . . .
From the desire of being honored, . . .
From the desire of being praised, . . .
From the desire of being preferred to others, . . .
From the desire of being consulted, . . .
From the desire of being approved, . . .
From the fear of being humiliated, . . .
From the fear of being despised, . . .
From the fear of suffering rebukes, . . .
From the fear of being calumniated, . . .
From the fear of being forgotten, . . .
From the fear of being ridiculed, . . .

From the fear of being wronged, . . .
From the fear of being suspected, . . .

That others may be loved more than I, **Jesus, grant me the grace to desire it.**
That others may be esteemed more than I, . . .
That, in the opinion of the world, others may increase and I may decrease, . . .
That others may be chosen and I set aside, . . .
That others may be praised and I unnoticed, . . .
That others may be preferred to me in everything, . . .
That others may become holier than I, provided that I may become as holy as I should, . . .
Amen.

I printed out several copies of the prayer and set them around my home and office. Then I conveniently forgot to pray it for the next three days.

Still, it kept nagging me. Every time I saw it, I swear, that sheet of paper looked up at me and said, "Here I am, lady. And I am on to you!"

Once I began the litany, however, something surprising started to happen: as unlikely as it sounds, I started to crave it. There wasn't just humility in that prayer, there was freedom too, and so much joy.

The author, Rafael Cardinal Merry del Val, was secretary of state for Pope St. Pius X, and it is rumored that Pius said the prayer every day. In today's culture, driven by bravado and loud opinions, where notoriety is a virtue and meekness derided,

where civility has been abandoned for savagery, the litany is a
mouthful. In it we plead for the grace to be forgotten, hidden,
even humiliated for the sake of Christ. We beg to go unnoticed so that others may win awards and accolades. We even
ask for that most difficult of graces: freedom from the fear of
being maliciously misrepresented or falsely accused. We truly,
radically ask for the willingness to suffer what Jesus suffered.

We have seen this kind of humility again and again in the
marvelous women in this book.

My director pointed out something important regarding
the litany: in order to pray it effectively, you should only pray
it after you have recollected yourself in the love of God—we
could say, only once you have placed yourself in the magnanimity of God, seeking what is great and striving to be worthy
of such a tremendous lover. When you are acutely aware of
God's deep affection and care for you, of your own nobility as
his daughter and heir, the litany seems like a relief. It's spiritual
common sense, a method to help you achieve freedom—the
freedom to do all the Father would ask and to allow yourself
to be entirely loved by him. That's quite a return.

This was something the women in these pages knew in their
bones: they were loved, *and* they were made for greatness in
God alone. They were unafraid of their littleness because they
knew God's magnanimity, and they stepped into his greatness
of heart as though stepping into a rushing, powerful river. They
allowed themselves to be carried along on his love and grace
to spectacular destinations.

This was what made it possible for them to suffer greatly
without losing themselves. This is what enabled them to share

profoundly in the cross of Jesus Christ, to hold humility and magnanimity in beautiful and perfect tension and to flourish as a result. This may be the most important lesson that they teach us. They reach out from these pages, waving their banners of virtue, saying, "Oh, my sisters, let us seek what is truly great and become worthy of it!"

Sisters, never doubt the import of your presence—to one another, to your families, to the world. A holy, deep-thinking woman present to the world can effect a spiritual leap of hope—like John leaping in Elizabeth's womb. A holy woman announces the presence of Jesus. She instills not human optimism but divine hope, with the power to cut through any barrier—slavery, loss, poverty, illness, disability, abuse, debauchery, calumny, distraction, loneliness, stupidity, ignorance, even full-out hate. A woman who brings Christ to the world through her presence and virtue is a dangerous and effective weapon against a culture of death, a culture that lacks the awareness of nobility, the magnanimity within its grasp—through Christ.

As you leave these pages, you may forget some of the stories, some of the details, but never forget your sacred lineage. Go forward to walk as companions with others on the road to a more virtuous life, confident of God's help. Welcome the support of the great Companion and of the multitude of holy women he has raised up as witnesses.

Exhaust them with your prayers. They can take it.

Live in nobility. Be a daughter of the King. Be present, be dangerous, and flourish for Jesus.

FOR JOURNALING

1. Are you thinking about humility in a new way? How?
2. Choosing one or two of the women from the previous chapters, describe how they embodied humility and magnanimity. What does this teach you about your own life?
3. How is ambition different from magnanimity? How is shame different from humility?
4. Write your own *Magnificat*: what are the great works that the Lord has done for you? Keep the list handy, and continually add to it.
5. What is one area of your life where you would like to really shine for Jesus? To seek the greatest, most virtuous response? Talk to Jesus about this desire for greatness in him.

FOR PRAYER

Through the intercession of the saint of your choice, pray for greater humility.

1. **Sirach 3:17—29:** Be humble in everything you do.
2. **Isaiah 57:14—21:** I dwell with the humble.
3. **Micah 6:6—8:** Live humbly with our God.
4. **Mark 9:33—37:** Be servant to all the rest.
5. **Philippians 2:1—11:** Consider others better than yourself.
6. **John 13:1—20:** Washing of the feet

7. **Matthew 6:1—6:** Do good in private.

8. **John 1:19—28:** Not fit to untie his sandal

Through the intercession of the saint of your choice, pray for greater magnanimity.

1. **Genesis 39:2—6:** The greatness of Joseph
2. **Daniel 3:26—28:** Happy to recount the works of the Lord
3. **Wisdom 13:5:** Beauty and greatness of created things
4. **1 Thessalonians 1:4:** He has chosen you.
5. **Psalm 145:1—6:** I will declare your greatness.
6. **1 Peter 2:9:** You are a chosen race.
7. **Matthew 18:1—5:** Who is the greatest?
8. **Luke 12:7:** You are of more value than many sparrows.

APPENDIX A: THE PROCESS OF CANONIZATION [185]

Servant of God -- the title given to a candidate for sainthood whose cause is still under investigation, prior to being declared Venerable.

Venerable – the title given to a candidate for sainthood whose cause has not yet reached the beatification stage but whose heroic virtue has been declared by the pope.

Beatification -- the second stage in the process of proclaiming a person a saint; occurs after a diocese or eparchy and the Congregation for the Causes of Saints has conducted a rigorous investigation into the person's life and writings to determine whether he or she demonstrates a heroic level of virtue, offered their life or suffered martyrdom. A miracle attributed to the person's intercession must be proved.

Blessed -- title bestowed on a person who has been beatified and accorded limited liturgical veneration.

Canonization – the formal process by which the Church declares a person to be a saint and worthy of universal veneration.

Saint – the title given to someone who has been formally canonized by the Church as sharing eternal life with God, and therefore offered for public veneration and imitation.

Appendix B: A Simple Guide to Praying with Scripture

- I ask the Holy Spirit to lead my meditation and invite Jesus to sit with me as I pray.
- I read over the verse for several minutes, repeating the passage slowly or even aloud if that is helpful.
- Where am I drawn, to what word or phrase or image? I rest there.
- What thoughts, feelings, or desires accompany this word or phrase or image? I name them.
- What is my response as the beauty and truth of this passage penetrates my heart? What is most prominent in my heart?

Notes

1. Jean-Pierre de Caussade, *Abandonment to Divine Providence* (Mineola, NY: Dover Publications, 2008 [1921]), 62.
2. Wilfrid Stinnesen, *Into Your Hands, Father: Abandoning Ourselves to the God Who Loves Us*, trans. Sister Clare Marie, OCD (San Francisco: Ignatius Press, 2011), 71–72, emphasis in the original.
3. John Wickham, SJ, *The Real Presence of the Future Kingdom: Scripture Passages for Daily Prayer on the Christian Virtues* (Montreal: Ignatian Centre Publications, 1990), 57, emphasis in the original.
4. Charette was appointed a captain of the Pontifical Zouaves, who protected the Papal States.
5. *Anne: The Life of Venerable Anne de Guigné*, by a Benedictine Nun of Stanbrook Abbey (Charlotte, NC: Tan Books, 1997), 3. This account of Anne's life is charming and one of the more thorough works available in multiple languages.
6. *Anne*, 5–6.
7. *Anne*, 9.
8. Venerable Anne of Guigné, accessed January 25, 2021, http://www.therealpresence.org/eucharst/mir/emc_book003_pdf/e_mir_st_children_91_92.pdf.
9. *Anne*, 17–18.

10. "Anne de Guigné," CatholicTradition.org, accessed February 2, 2021, http://www.catholictradition.org/Children/anne-guigne3.htm.
11. *Anne*, 53.
12. *Anne*, 43.
13. *Anne*, 67.
14. *Anne*, 85.
15. *Anne*, 88–89.
16. *Anne*, 94.
17. *Anne*, 99.
18. *Anne*, 63.
19. *Anne*, 63.
20. *Anne*, 64.
21. Sr. Jane Dominic Laurel, OP, "Suffering and the Narrative of Redemption," *National Catholic Bioethics Quarterly*, 17, no. 3 (Autumn 2017): 437–59.
22. Wickham, *The Real Presence of the Future Kingdom*, 82.
23. Wickham, 82.
24. Wickham, 84.
25. Wickham, 84.
26. I am indebted to Francesca Dammerman for an abundance of materials on the life of Benedetta in English.
27. Dom Antoine Marie, OSB, "Venerable Benedetta Bianchi Porro," Saint Joseph de Clairval Abbey Newsletter (Flavigny, France), January 21, 2011, https://www.clairval.com/index.php/en/letter/?id=2190111.
28. *Beyond Silence: Life Diary Letters of Benedetta Bianchi Porro*, published by Benedetta's friends and translated by Mother Agnes with David Giddings. Date unknown.
29. *Beyond Silence*, 30.
30. Catholic Saints Info, https://catholicsaints.info/blessed-benedetta-bianchi-porro/, accessed January 26, 2021.

31. *Beyond Silence*, 13.
32. *Beyond Silence*, 13.
33. Dom Antoine Marie, "Venerable Benedetta Bianchi Porro."
34. Dom Antoine Marie.
35. *Beyond Silence*, 42.
36. *Beyond Silence*, 86.
37. Dom Antoine Marie.
38. Dom Antoine Marie.
39. Dom Antoine Marie.
40. Dom Antoine Marie.
41. Dom Antoine Marie.
42. Dom Antoine Marie.
43. *Beyond Silence*, 19.
44. *Beyond Silence*, 19.
45. *Beyond Silence*, 55
46. Francis de Sales, *Introduction to the Devout Life,* part 3, chap. 19, www.oblates.org.
47. *Beyond Silence*, 40.
48. *Beyond Silence*, 57.
49. *Beyond Silence*, 95–96.
50. *Beyond Silence*, 70–71.
51. *Beyond Silence*, 81.
52. Dom Antoine Marie.
53. Dom Antoine Marie.
54. Carlo Carretto, *Letters from the Desert*, trans. Rose Mary Hancock (Maryknoll, NY: Orbis Books, 1972), 130–31.
55. Susan Szalewski, "Recently Beatified Young Woman Demonstrated Value of Suffering," Catholic Voice, June 11, 2020, https://catholicvoiceomaha.com/recently-beati-fied-young-woman-demonstrated-value-of-suffering/.

56. *Beyond Silence*, 55.
57. "Blessed Benedetta Bianchi Porro," CatholicSaints.Info, accessed January 29, 2021, https://catholicsaints.info/blessed-benedetta-bianchi-porro/.
58. Translation by Mike Munford, found at Konstantin Siminov: Siminov through English Eyes, https://simonov.co.uk/waitforme, used with permission.
59. Romano Guardini, *Learning the Virtues That Lead You to God* (Manchester, NH: Sophia, 1998), 44.
60. Guardini, *Learning the Virtues That Lead You to God*, 26.
61. Guardini, 43.
62. Anonymous author, *Blessed Elizabeth Canori Mora: Mother and Mystic*, trans. Mary Elizabeth Herbert (Post Falls, ID: Mediatrix Press, 2018), xiii.
63. From the US Conference of Catholic Bishops: The heroic life of Blessed Elizabeth Canori Mora should not be taken as a suggestion of a course of action or a model for any given woman in a situation of domestic abuse, except in her perseverance in charity. In the time in which she lived, Blessed Elizabeth had little choice in terms of domestic arrangement, but she was able to cope with her suffering in an extraordinary way. The Bishops' document "When I Call for Help" has advice for women today who experience domestic violence. Violence in a relationship is never healthy, as detailed at the For Your Marriage website, and thankfully women today can receive the help they deserve both for themselves and for their children to be safe. See http://www.marriageuniqueforareason.org/2012/02/09/national-marriage-week-an-example-of-faithful-love-enduring-unto-death-bl-elizabeth-canori-mora/.

64. *Blessed Elizabeth*, 5.

65. Cited in Eugene Hemrick, "Acceptance: A Lesson in the Virtue of Realism," The National Institute for the Renewal of the Priesthood, June 1, 2016, http://www.jknirparchive.com/acceptance.html.

66. *Blessed Elizabeth*, 10.

67. *Blessed Elizabeth*, 14.

68. *Blessed Elizabeth*, 15.

69. *Blessed Elizabeth*, 36.

70. *Blessed Elizabeth*, 37.

71. *Blessed Elizabeth*, 147.

72. *Blessed Elizabeth*, 147.

73. Pope John Paul II, Homily from the Beatification Mass of Elizabeth Canori Mora, April 1994.

74. *Blessed Elizabeth*, 149.

75. *Blessed Elizabeth*, 145.

76. Guardini, *Learning the Virtues That Lead You to God*, 181.

77. Guardini, 176.

78. Guardini, 176

79. Guardini, 181.

80. Robert Cardinal Sarah, *The Power of Silence: Against the Dictatorship of Noise,* with Nicolas Diat (San Francisco: Ignatius Press, 2017), 56.

81. This phrase is from David Meconi, ed., *Catherine de Hueck Doherty: Essential Writings* (Maryknoll, NY: Orbis Books, 2009).

82. Meconi, *Catherine de Hueck Doherty,* 22.

83. Catherine Doherty: *In the Footprints of Loneliness* (Combermere, ON: Madonna House Publications, 2003), 51.

84. Meconi, 34.

85. Catherine Doherty, *Poustinia: Encountering God in Silence, Solitude and Prayer* (Combermere, ON: Madonna House Publications, 1993), 8.
86. Doherty, 14.
87. Doherty, 21. Italics in the original.
88. Doherty, 24–25.
89. Meconi, 38.
90. Doherty, *Poustinia*, 5.
91. Doherty, 51.
92. Doherty, 4-5.
93. Doherty, 97.
94. Wickham 5, emphasis mine.
95. Pope Benedict XVI, *The Yes of Jesus Christ: Spiritual Exercises in Faith, Hope, and Love* (New York, NY; Crossroads, 1991), 34.
96. Benedict XVI, 34.
97. Roberto Italo Zanini, *Bakhita: From Slave to Saint*, trans. Andrew Matt (San Francisco: Ignatius Press, 2013), 30. Zanini's book is painstakingly researched, offering an extensive reflection on the complex history and culture of this period so deeply entrenched in the slave trade and its effects on the people of that region that are felt intensely even today.
98. Zanini, 38-39.
99. Zanini, 40-41.
100. Zanini, 49.
101. Zanini, 60-61.
102. Zanini, 62.
103. Zanini, 79.
104. Zanini, 93.
105. Zanini, 137.

106. Zanini, 83.
107. Zanini, 81.
108. Zanini, 88.
109. Zanini, 89.
110. Guardini, *Learning the Virtues That Lead You to God*, 105.
111. Wickham, 75, *The Real Presence of the Future Kingdom*, emphasis mine.
112. Wickham, 78.
113. Wickham, 77.
114. Wickham, 77.
115. Zanini, *Bakhita*, 140.
116. Zanini, 141.
117. Zanini, 141.
118. As quoted in Zanini, 160.
119. Homily of John Paul II for the Canonization of 123 New Saints, October 1, 2000, 5, http://www.vatican.va/content/john-paul-ii/en/homilies/2000/documents/hf_jp-ii_hom_20001001_canonization.html.
120. Zanini, 25.
121. Zanini, 138.
122. Zanini, 114.
123. Josef Pieper, *Faith, Hope, Love* (San Francisco: Ignatius Press, 1991), 103.
124. Pieper, 105.
125. As quoted in Pieper, 105.
126. Wickham, *The Real Presence of the Future Kingdom*, 101.
127. I am indebted to my friend Mandy Z. for her generous supply of materials on St. Mary MacKillop direct from Australia.

128. Paul Gardiner, SJ, *The Virtues of Saint Mary of the Cross, Mary MacKillop, 1842-1909* (Strathfield, Australia: St. Paul's Publications, 2017), 16.
129. Gardiner, 17.
130. Gardiner, 17.
131. Paul Gardiner, SJ, *An Extraordinary Australian: Mary MacKillop, The Authorised Biography* (North Sydney, Australia: David Ell Publishing, 1993), 32.
132. Gardiner, *The Virtues*, 124.
133. Gardiner, 143.
134. Gardiner, *An Extraordinary Australian*, 21.
135. Gardiner, 41.
136. Gardiner, 53.
137. Gardiner, 86.
138. Gardiner, 140.
139. Gardiner, 19.
140. Gardiner, 38.
141. Fr. Gardiner's authoritative biography of St. Mary is researched with exquisite care and attention to the many nuances at play in this episode and other trials in St. Mary's life.
142. Gardiner, *The Virtues*, 23.
143. Gardiner, *An Extraordinary Australian*, 287.
144. Gardiner, 265.
145. Gardiner, *The Virtues*, 25.
146. Gardiner, 46.
147. Gardiner, *An Extraordinary Australian*, 305.
148. Gardiner, 284.

149. Homily of His Holiness, Benedict XVI, Mass for the Canonization of New Saints, October 17, 2010, http://www.vatican.va/content/benedict-xvi/en/homilies/2010/documents/hf_ben-xvi_hom_20101017_canonizations.html.
150. Gardiner, 48.
151. Gardiner, 41.
152. Gardiner, 47.
153. Pieper, *Faith, Hope, Love*, 179.
154. Benedict XVI, *The Yes of Jesus Christ*, 70.
155. Benedict XVI, 104-105.
156. Benedict XVI, 114-115.
157. Charlotte Kelly, "A Saint of the Stage, Eve Lavallière," accessed January 30, 2021, https://www.ecatholic2000.com/cts/untitled-09.shtml.
158. Kelly.
159. John Murray, "Eve Lavallière," CatholicIreland.net, November 30, 1999, https://www.catholicireland.net/eve-lavalliere/.
160. Kelly, "A Saint of the Stage."
161. Kelly.
162. Kelly.
163. As quoted in Jennifer Ristine, *Mary Magdalene: Insights from Ancient Magdala* (Magdala, Israel: Magdalena Institute, 2018), 101. Ristine's book is a wonderful resource on the various legends and traditions that grew up around Mary Magdalene. She parses them out, one by one, with great clarity.
164. Jean Baptiste Henri D. Lacordaire, *St. Mary Magdalen*, trans. E. A. Hazeland (London: Burns and Oates, 1880), 14–19. This version is housed in the Bodlein Library at Oxford and is missing pages 101–14.

165. Lacordaire, 215.

166. Christopher L. C. E. Witcombe, "Investigating Mary Magdalen," accessed January 31, 2021, http://arthistoryresources.net/investigating-mary-magdalen/mm-gregory-homily-33.html.

167. Witcombe.

168. Lacordaire, *St. Mary Magdalen*, 12-13.

169. Kelly, "A Saint of the Stage."

170. Kelly.

171. Kelly.

172. Kelly.

173. Kelly.

174. Kelly.

175. Kelly.

176. Benedict XVI, *The Yes of Jesus Christ*, 90.

177. Kelly, "A Saint of the Stage."

178. Kelly.

179. Kelly.

180. Lacordaire, *St. Mary Magdalen*, 217.

181. Pieper, *Faith, Hope, Love*, 102.

182. Josef Pieper, *A Brief Reader on the Virtues of the Human Heart* (San Francisco: Ignatius Press, 1991), 37.

183. Pope Benedict XVI, Homily for the Beginning of the Petrine Ministry, St. Peter's Square, April 24, 2005, http://www.vatican.va/content/benedict-xvi/en/homilies/2005/documents/hf_ben-xvi_hom_20050424_inizio-pontificato.html.

184. Fr. Cajetan Mary da Bergamo, *Humility of Heart*, trans. Herbert Cardinal Vaughan (Charlotte, NC: Tan Books, 2011), 1.

185. Adapted from the United States Conference of Catholic Bishops.

ABOUT THE AUTHOR

L iz Kelly is a popular speaker and an award-winning author of nine books, including *Reasons I Love Being Catholic*, which won the Catholic Press Association First Place award for Best Popular Presentation of the Faith in 2007, and *Jesus Approaches: What Contemporary Women Can Learn about Healing, Freedom and Joy from the Women of the New Testament*, which has won a number of awards, including Best Book in the Religion/Christianity category for 2017-2019. Her written works frequently appear in the Magnificat's Lenten and Advent Companions and in other Catholic venues, including Catholic Spirit, Blessed is She, and Jesuitprayer.org.

Her monthly column, Your Heart, His Home, is published throughout the US. Kelly has appeared on Relevant Radio, Catholic Answers, Radio Maria, Public Radio, Boston Catholic Television, EWTN, and Salt and Light Television. She is presently the managing editor of *Logos: A Journal of Catholic Thought and Culture*, published through the Center for Catholic Studies at the University of St. Thomas and cohost along with David Deavel of the podcast, Deep Down Things (deepdownthings/ patreon.com). She and her husband, Vincent, an architect, live in Minnesota. Find out more at LizK.org.

Praise for *Jesus Approaches*

"This book has helped ignite my prayer life at a time when I didn't even realize the flame was low. It breathed fresh life into Gospel stories I thought I knew inside and out. Moreover, it brought these stories into my life, speaking to me personally in ways I've seldom experienced."~Elizabeth E.

"An immense gift for women. With vulnerability and grace . . . *Jesus Approaches* is a perfect balance of Scriptural reflection and personal testimony, all woven into stirring accounts of women in the New Testament."~Kelsey W., St. Paul, MN

"Simply beautiful, and a must for every Christian woman . . . I devoured this book immediately . . . and I can't wait to go back through it slowly, chew on it, use it as a devotional tool, and meditate on the prayers and verses at each chapter's end."~Evangeline W., New York, NY

"I had big hopes when I picked up this book and I wasn't disappointed! I felt like I made wonderful new friends in both the author and in the women of the Bible to whom she introduced to me. Most importantly, her reflections and invitation to have my own, led me to deep encounters with Jesus that were very special to my heart."~Amazon reviewer, Kindle edition